PENGUIN BOOKS

## THE NEW INDIA

Ved Mehta was born in India in 1934 but has lived in
the West since 1949; he became an American citizen
in 1975. He holds degrees from Pomona College,
from Oxford University, where he read in the Honours School of Modern History at Balliol College,
and from Harvard University. His first book was published in 1957, and since then he has written many
others and contributed hundreds of articles and stories
to British, Indian, and American publications, primarily *The New Yorker.* His books, which have appeared
in dozens of translations and editions, encompass an
autobiography *(Face to Face);* a travel journal *(Walking
the Indian Streets);* reports on contemporary philoso-
phy and historiography *(Fly and the Fly-Bottle),* on contemporary Christian theology *(The New Theologian),*
and on transformational grammar *(John Is Easy to
Please);* a novel *(Delinquent Chacha);* a biography
*(Daddyji);* and a study of a country trying to modern-
ize itself *(Portrait of India).* Ved Mehta's most recent
book is *Mahatma Gandhi and His Apostles,* also published by Penguin Books.

# The
# NEW
# India

## VED MEHTA

PENGUIN BOOKS

Penguin Books Ltd, Harmondsworth,
Middlesex, England
Penguin Books, 625 Madison Avenue,
New York, New York 10022, U.S.A.
Penguin Books Australia Ltd, Ringwood,
Victoria, Australia
Penguin Books Canada Limited, 2801 John Street,
Markham, Ontario, Canada L3R 1B4
Penguin Books (N.Z.) Ltd, 182–190 Wairau Road,
Auckland 10, New Zealand

First published in the United States of America in
simultaneous hardcover and paperback editions by
The Viking Press and Penguin Books 1978
First published in Great Britain in Penguin Books 1978
Reprinted 1978

LIBRARY OF CONGRESS CATALOGING IN PUBLICATION DATA
Mehta, Ved Parkash.
The new India.
Includes index.
1. India—Politics and government—1947-
I. Title.
DS480.84.M38 1977b    320.9'54'05    77-21440
ISBN 0 14 00.4570 8

Printed in the United States of America by
Offset Paperback Mfrs., Inc., Dallas, Pennsylvania
Set in Videocomp Garamond

The contents of this book originally appeared in
*The New Yorker* in a somewhat different form.

TO THE MEMORY OF IVAN MORRIS

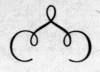

# Contents

# PROLOGUE

## *New Delhi, 1974-75*

There is a sense of looming calamity here, a sense of danger. One morning, in my parents' house, I am greeted by the news that the cleaning woman has been electrocuted while hanging the wash on a wire clothesline strung between two lampposts, which had been rained on during the night. The same night, a pig rampaged through the garden, and gave birth there to seventeen piglets. The garden is in ruins and the stench unbearable, and no one knows what to do. The pig (and its piglets) may belong to one of the Untouchable sweepers who camp out in the back lanes. The pig may be his only worldly possession, and if anything should happen to it there might be a sweepers' riot. Indeed, I hear rumors all the time of murders and of riots touched off by religious or caste conflicts. I read in the newspapers that the government is going easy on the rioters—especially those from militant minority groups—because it is afraid that it will not be able to stop the riots from spreading. I hear reports of intimidation and corrupt practices in high and low places, of knifing incidents and hooliganism in the streets and on the buses, of servants becoming restive. I've been visiting India every year for many years now. Each year, fear, corruption, and violence have increased, but this year they seem to have become a way of life.

A friend tells me that a while ago her male cook, who had

served her family well for twenty years, suddenly became rude and truculent. She suspected that he was spitting in the food. The family were afraid of what he might do if they dismissed him, but finally, two months ago, they did. Since then, their house has been burglarized twice. They have three Alsatian watchdogs, yet the burglar (or burglars) has been able to get in and out undetected. The family had long since stopped keeping anything valuable in the house—not so much as a silver tray or a gold chain—but the burglar has somehow managed to find whatever money was there, and the family is full of foreboding.

I dine in the flat of a senior government official. He comes downstairs to see me off. No sooner have I reached home than I get a call from his wife saying that he hasn't returned. She fears he's been kidnapped. As it turns out, he has only gone around the corner to buy cigarettes—something he must have done hundreds of times before, when things were more normal.

A few days after undergoing some minor surgery, I drive out to the Holy Family Hospital to have the stitches removed. On the way back, a little boy darts into the road in front of the car. The driver brakes, and we stop a few inches short of the boy. The boy, who is perhaps eight years old, stumbles and falls and starts screaming with fright. A hundred children rush over from a nearby school, climb onto the hood and the trunk, and pound on the windows shouting, "Police! Police! This car has hurt our brother!" Grownups join the children and start threatening the driver, demanding money and revenge. It takes us more than an hour to persuade them that the child was not hurt and to let us drive on. The driver tells me that in Calcutta the police advise drivers not to stop after an accident but to get to the nearest police station as soon as they can. In an incident like the one we were involved in, apparently, a Calcutta crowd would set fire to the car. So things in New Delhi are at least better than things in Calcutta.

New Delhi is in the throes of perhaps the worst outbreak of nationalism and xenophobia it has ever known—directed almost entirely against the West. Itinerant Western hippies are reviled for choosing to be as dirty as Untouchables. Western missionaries are decried for turning the Indian poor into misfits in their own society by converting them to Christianity. Visiting Western scholars are condemned for using their greater financial and material resources to dominate Indian studies and for displaying "colonial," "exploitative," and "patronizing" attitudes toward their Indian colleagues. Western volunteer workers are viewed either as dupes or as C.I.A. agents. Working conditions here for Westerners have been made so difficult that most of them have gone home, including many valuable agronomists and technical experts. The Rockefeller Foundation, which for fifty years was famous in India for its medical and agricultural work, has cut back its operations and closed down its New Delhi office.

The few remaining Western diplomats, journalists, executives of philanthropic organizations, and volunteer workers—many of them Americans—now live and work mostly in isolation, both from one another and from the Indians they have come to serve. These Westerners have little in common with the old-time India-lovers—European students of Indian history and religion; travellers; gazetteers—who wrote some of the best books ever written on India. The newcomers are often decent people, but they don't know India. They seem always to be taken by surprise by the twists and turns of the Indian mind and by caste prejudices and other religious idiosyncrasies. They seek to counteract their ignorance by cultivating indifference, which can mean ceasing to trust their most ordinary human impulses—for instance, hesitating to offer a glass of water to their driver for fear of offending some caste convention. A recent remark made by a high-ranking American diplomat suggests the extent of these Westerners' ignorance: "If the average Indian had to choose between going hungry and his country's not having nuclear bombs, he would choose nuclear bombs." Western institutions such as the Ford Foundation and the embassies occupy modern, air-conditioned buildings that are equipped with filtered hot and cold running water and private swimming pools, and are set in well-cared-for, lush green grounds. Once, these buildings and grounds served as examples of modern elegance to which Indians could aspire, but now to the same Indians they have become embarrassing symbols of unattainable affluence. In the nineteen-fifties and early nineteen-sixties, Western journalists in India had a strong emotional involvement with the country, often referring to it as "the great adventure in Western-style democracy." They have been succeeded by detached or disdainful observers, who have been known to call India things like "a permanent basket case." Western diplomats do not seek the company of Indians as they used to. And Indians, in turn, neither covet invitations to Western embassies nor prize the presence of the Western ambassadors at their social and academic functions as they used to. One observer of Indian-American relations has said, "You know that the American ambassador has a dog. But the American dog has not met a single Indian dog in the eighteen months it has been here. That's about the state of Indian-American relations right now." The American diplomats and the executives of philanthropic organizations used to work in concert, but now they are at loggerheads. World Bank people say that the Ford Foundation has a colonial outlook. Ford Foundation people say that the American Embassy has nothing but contempt for India and things Indian. American Embassy people say that the Ford Foundation leads the Indian government to believe that in seeking aid it can bypass the Administration in Washington and appeal directly to a constituency made up of Harvard University, the New York *Times,* and the Senate Foreign Relations Committee. And those few wrangling Westerners who don't take refuge in defensive cynicism go to the other extreme and become aggressively pro-Indian. They deplore the gloom-and-doom Westerners, and say things like "I'm tired of hearing Westerners say 'India is no God-damned good, the government is no God-damned good, Prime Minister Indira Gandhi is no God-damned good.' " They call for "positivistic" thinking—in other words, for dealing with what is, here and now, and letting India's future take care of itself. They are likely to be invited to the homes of Westernized Indians to eat from "a Mongolian firepot"—the current rage—which is many kinds of food boiled together in a pot at the table.

The talk at such gatherings is apt to be a little glib, a little cosmopolitan, and a little risqué. At one gathering, a Westernized Indian tells me, "I have a wonderful Untouchable sweeper, but I would never let him into my house. I have no objection to sitting and even eating with him at my table—it's just that he has filthy Untouchable habits."

I overhear another Westernized Indian say, "The only possible response to the conditions here is to go around with a Martini in one hand and a grenade in the other."

All the other guests agree with him.

Soon they are all listening to a deaf painter, the brother of a Minister in Mrs. Gandhi's Cabinet, who is renowned for his fund of stories. "The Marquess of Linlithgow, our erstwhile Viceroy, was a great lover of cattle shows," he says. "One day, he and Lady Linlithgow went to the great cattle show in New Delhi. When they got there, they wandered off in different directions. A Punjabi rustic with a huge bull approached Lady Linlithgow and said to her, 'This is the greatest bull in all India.' 'How do you know?' Lady Linlithgow asked. 'He can satisfy a cow two dozen times a day,' the man with the bull said. 'Go and tell my husband that,' she said. When the man found Lord Linlithgow, he repeated his praise of the bull and told him what Lady Linlithgow had said. 'But is it the same cow, my man?' Lord Linlithgow asked."

Indians and Westerners roar with delight.

Westernized Indian society in New Delhi is made up of high-ranking government officials and politicians, members of the professions, and occasional migrants from Calcutta or Bombay society. Its worst term of opprobrium, "new money," or "nouveau riche," is applied to people who have made their money since independence, in 1947, and its highest praise, "old money," is reserved for people who made their money before independence. New Delhi society has been humming with news of the

engagement of Sanjay Gandhi, who is Mrs. Gandhi's son, to
Menaka Anand, a professional model, who was recently featured
in a story in the English-language *Hindustan Times* headlined
"From Towels and Mattresses to Maruti." Maruti is the name of
a "people's car" that Sanjay Gandhi has been licensed by the
government to manufacture and sell, over the protests of Mrs.
Gandhi's political opponents, who accuse her of family favoritism.
The newspaper story, after describing how Miss Anand got her
start in towel advertising, goes on:

> Menaka joined Lady Sri Ram College to do a Political
> Science (Honours) course that she dropped later. There at
> the Miss Fresher [beauty] contest . . . asked to compose an
> impromptu nursery rhyme, she came up with this cameo:

> > "The man in the moon,
> > Looked out of the moon,
> > Looked out of the moon and said:
> > 'The world's so dizzy,
> > Everyone is in a tizzy,
> > I'm glad I'm not human,
> > I'd rather be dead!' "

> Naturally enough Menaka won the crown. (The *Evening
> News* "discovered" young Menaka in a front-page story on
> the event, Aug. 23, 1973.) . . .

> Soon enough a mattress company signed her on to model
> for them. (She wears a nightie. . . .) Menaka was famous
> overnight. . . .

> Menaka then decided to migrate to journalism (warms
> the poor journalists' cockles, no?). She enrolled herself in
> Sam Castelino's "Dateline School of Journalism." . . .

> Her tutors at the school wistfully remember how she had
> got late one evening and they gave her a lift home. On the
> way she suggested she interview Sanjay Gandhi! Not know-
> ing how well she knew him, the tutor casually remarked,
> "Yes, but find out if he's willing to be interviewed."

"I'm meeting him this evening," Menaka softly replied. She never went to the school again!!

Cultural interchange in the capital seems to be limited at present to talk about the young couple or to lectures on some such fashionable topic as the lure of the occult, India's economic plight, or how much better things are in China than they are in India. A few months back, a dance program or a vocal or sitar recital could always be found and would be well attended. But fewer people can now get to such events in either private cars or taxis, because of the ever-increasing price of gasoline. (New Delhi has a notoriously bad public transportation system.) For the same reason, social gatherings of all kinds have become smaller and rarer. The well-to-do Westernized Indian men go less frequently to their clubs after work for tennis, swimming, or cards. Their wives have curtailed their morning coffee parties in restaurants and also what they call their "kitty" parties—gatherings that usually involve a couple of dozen wives, who take turns entertaining the group at lunch, at which time a little lottery is held. Everyone puts a set sum in a kitty, and then all draw lots for it. Matters are so arranged that sooner or later everyone gets the kitty. Such parties used to be occasions for minor feasts, but the menus are now often restricted to one savory dish and one sweet dish.

During the monsoon season, which generally runs from early July to the middle of September, the sky is streaked with heavy clouds, and there are heavy rains. New Delhi is verdant. The trees have burst into yellow, purple, and orange blossom. Lush, tall flowers, especially snapdragons, are almost everywhere. The fountains are gushing. The accumulated dust of summer has been washed away from the ruins of earlier cities, from the faded Mogul monuments, from the magnificent, stately buildings put up by the British, from the occasional tall, modern buildings, from ancient stones and modern bricks, from every leaf of every tree. No matter how heavy the downpour, people go about without umbrellas or protection of any kind, as if they were amphibians. They dress in bright-colored clothes, and the air is filled with the hum of insects and the calls of large, brilliant birds. Because of the dampness, all sorts of things must now be kept in tight jars or tins; otherwise biscuits become limp, salt and sugar turn into rocks, matches won't light—the heads simply fall off, even off matches specially treated for the monsoon. Clothes won't dry, and they always smell a little damp, even after they have been ironed. Telephones don't work; cars stall. The network of open drains overflows, flooding the streets.

Lying between the sacred river Jumna and an outcrop of the Aravalli Hills is the Delhi plain, on which New Delhi stands. Legend and history tell us that on various sites on this plain more than ten other cities once stood: Indraprastha, in the tenth century B.C., or maybe it was the fifteenth; Dilli, around the first century B.C.; Lal Kot, in the eleventh century A.D.; Kila Rai Pathora, in the twelfth century; Siri, Tughlakabad, Jahanpannah, and Firuzabad, all in the fourteenth century; Dinepannah, in the sixteenth century; Shahjahanabad, in the seventeenth century; and what is now called Old Delhi, which has something of all of them in it. It has old Muslim tombs and British gardens, old Hindu temples and Protestant churches, old Mogul battlements and British barracks, old mosques and towers, old city walls and gates, old mean streets and bazaars. In alcoves in the ancient walls, on the steps that go down to the Jumna River, Brahmans chant Sanskrit verses, as other Brahmans have done for more than three thousand years. In Chandni Chowk, or Silver Street, in the shadow of the Jama Masjid, one of the world's great mosques, goldsmiths and silversmiths sell bangles and baubles, as their forebears did in the days of the Mogul emperors, and brasher venders offer roast kabobs and Coca-Cola. In the Red Fort, once the residence of Shah Jahan himself, guides tell how he built Shahjahanabad here and the Taj Mahal in Agra. Still living in elegant, if crumbling, quarters are the old high-caste Delhi wallahs, descendants of courtiers proverbially loyal in their service to Hindu, Muslim, or British rulers, always marrying within their own charmed circle. The area in

colonies—little neighborhoods or suburbs with their own bazaars, slums, and distinctive personalities—which sprang up to the
south and west at the time of the partition of India, when hundreds of thousands of Punjabi refugees flocked to New Delhi and
settled on land made available to them by the government in
partial compensation for their losses in Pakistan. Thanks largely
to the Punjabis, New Delhi is conspicuously more prosperous
than Old Delhi, Bombay, or Calcutta. The Punjabis have, in fact,
stamped their character on New Delhi. They are renowned for
hard work, an enterprising spirit, proud bearing, primitive, unsophisticated ways, an aggressive, rambunctious manner, hearty
appetites, and boastful talk. In the streets, Punjabi men are apt to
ogle women and to make their way through crowds with sly, wily,
hit-and-run shoves and pushes. At home, they like to sit and stare
into space and draw comfort from being with one another. It is
said that if a Punjabi gets a good meal three or four times a day
and a long nap in the afternoon he is content. The habit of reading
is almost unknown among the Punjabis, and they don't have
much use for art; their houses are decorated mostly with garish
calendars, brightly painted gods and goddesses, and family photo-
graphs—of revered or departed elders, of weddings or other
family events.

Both New and Old Delhi are breeding grounds for mosquitoes, flies, and vermin. The water-supply system is so erratic
and so badly maintained that as much as twenty-five per cent of
the water is lost through seepage. In Shahjahanabad and other
congested areas, some people rely for water on hand pumps that
tap the subsoil, which is contaminated by the rubbish and sewage
allowed to accumulate in lanes and by-lanes. As a consequence of
all this, according to one estimate, one out of five residents comes
down every year with a disease like dysentery, infectious hepati-
tis, malaria, cholera, or typhoid.

Most educated people here still get their news from three or four
English-language dailies of nationwide circulation, which report
mainly on conditions in the cities or on the doings of the central

which many of the original thick, high stone walls and gateways of Shahjahanabad still stand is now a crowded, stinking slum, with all sorts of cottage industries.

New Delhi, which was built three miles south of Shahjahanabad, dates from 1911, when the British transferred their capital here from Calcutta. Because of the strategic position of the Delhi plain, many of the cities here had served other dynasties as their capitals. Christopher Hussey, in his exhaustive biography of Sir Edwin Lutyens, the British architect who, with Sir Herbert Baker, designed the new capital, writes, "From the moment of its foundation the city evoked sectional antagonism, both English and Indian. The English community in Calcutta, seeing their city reduced . . . to provincial status, did not scruple to recall the superstition that Delhi is the graveyard of dynasties. Pointing to the six previous capitals whose ruins litter the plain around that of Shah Jahan, some foretold that the building of an eighth presaged likewise the end of British rule." The main buildings of the Imperial capital—the Viceroy's palace, Parliament House, the two blocks of the Secretariat, all of which are a mixture of Roman and Indian architecture—together with the big government bungalows, and their compounds and servants' quarters, still form the core of New Delhi, which since 1947 has been the capital of independent India. There are many open spaces—wide, tree-lined boulevards and traffic roundabouts planted with flowers—which are reminiscent of the grace and order of the British raj. The grounds of various monuments are well kept up and are free of squatters. Because there is no heavy industry in New Delhi, the city does not have poor laborers like those who camp in the streets of Old Delhi, Bombay, and Calcutta. Occasionally, when there is a road to be built, a few hundred laborers will camp at the site or start living in some of the huge sections of pipe that are to be laid down for the water supply. The New Delhi police are fairly strict about chasing away squatters and campers, because they want the capital to make a good impression on the foreigners who come here to work.

Grafted onto the elegant capital are scores of so-called

17

government here in the capital. Weeks often go by without the appearance of a single story from any of the six hundred thousand villages in which most of the people live. These dailies have an inbred character; the people who own them, the people who read them, and the people whose doings are chronicled in them all belong to the tiny middle-class élite who live in the few big cities and have a monopoly on literacy, property, money, and power. But all these papers are now in difficulties: the Delhi edition of the *Statesman* recently had to suspend publication for several months because of a labor dispute; the *Hindustan Times* is said to be feeling the financial pinch; the *Indian Express* is having editorial troubles; the *Times of India,* perhaps the best of the four, is now only eight pages thick, because of a shortage of paper, from which all are suffering. (The newspapers in the Indian vernaculars are weaker and smaller—pale copies of their English counterparts.) The government controls the supply of newsprint, and now the government has come to believe that reports of social unrest only cause more unrest, so the newspapers have to tread warily. Even so, they carry daily reports of food riots, administrative breakdowns, and students' and workers' strikes.

John Kenneth Galbraith once described India as "a functioning anarchy." If that is what it is, it is certainly an anarchy that functioned best after the establishment of the British raj, in 1858; the British are credited even by their critics with having unified India and imposed law and order upon it. The "Indianization" of India that has been going on since independence is becoming a kind of regression to the days before the raj. Old accounts of Indian intrigue, nepotism, and courts and courtiers written by European observers in the eighteenth and early nineteenth centuries bear an unnerving resemblance to what is happening now. Signs of backward-looking political and religious nationalism are everywhere. On All-India Radio, there are daily news broadcasts in Sanskrit. There is constant talk about the glories of ancient India—about how the Hindus in Vedic times travelled around in "flying machines," talked to each other on "skyphones," and constructed "bridges of stones" spanning oceans. The heroic feats

and the anthropomorphic characteristics of the *devas,* or gods, and *asuras,* or demons, in the ancient Hindu epics are being taken literally again. The foreign book most widely discussed among students at Delhi University is Erich von Däniken's "Chariots of the Gods." The students take it as proof that in antiquity not only India but also other parts of the world lived through a technological age more advanced than that of the present day in the West.

Seventy-five per cent of all Indians have no assured employment and earn four hundred rupees (about fifty-three dollars) or less a year. They cannot even count on such rock-bottom necessities for survival as one meal a day and one piece of permanent clothing, and so fall below what the Indian government has defined in its official income profile as "the poverty line." The top five per cent of all Indians have assured employment and earn forty-eight hundred rupees (six hundred and forty dollars) or more a year. This leaves about twenty per cent somewhere in between. A few years ago, I used to hear much fashionable talk about "the bourgeoisie," "the lower middle class," and "the upper middle class," as if the poor did not exist at all and the top five per cent—the only people to whom such class distinctions could conceivably apply—made up the entire country. Now I hear talk only about the well-to-do and the poor. And even the well-to-do talk about their children with uneasiness, as if the children were no longer securely above the poverty line but were in danger of being dragged into the vortex of destitution. Some college students fear for themselves also. Last year, many of them were going to college in buses and eating two *parathas,* or unleavened wheatcakes, at every meal. This year, they are walking to college and eating only one *paratha.*

Until rather recently, only the poor here woke up in the morning and asked themselves, "Will we eat today?" Now the well-to-do, who in a sense have always lived just to eat, are beginning to wonder how long they will go on waking up and asking themselves, "What shall we eat today?" There is a shortage of practically everything. The prices of rice, wheat, and sugar have doubled or quadrupled in the open market in a year, and the

# The
# NEW
*India*

# 1

# The Continent of Silence

India, the land of every seventh person in the world, became virtually a continent of silence on June 26, 1975, when Indira Gandhi's government proclaimed a state of emergency. One of Mrs. Gandhi's first acts of the Emergency—the blanket term for the proclamation itself and the stream of repressive measures and actions that followed it—was to issue an ordinance that made both Indian and foreign journalists subject to fines and imprisonment for publishing items deemed "objectionable" or "embarrassing" to the government or likely to "bring into hatred or contempt or excite disaffection toward the government . . . and thereby cause or tend to cause public disorder." After nineteen months came the "relaxed enforcement" of the Emergency, following a call by Mrs. Gandhi on January 18, 1977, for elections two months later. Nonetheless, the "publication of objectionable matter" ordinance, as it was known, remained in force. Under its provisions, in the early weeks of the Emergency many of the Western news, radio, and television organizations had been coerced into closing their bureaus and offices. The handful of Western journalists who were allowed to remain had to work under such stringent "press guidelines" that they soon began functioning as mere purveyors of government propaganda. When the Emergency was about two months old, William Borders, of the New York *Times,* filed a

prices of spices, cooking oils, and ghee are going up each month. Milk, bread, and butter have all become scarce, and such daily staples as wheat flour and corn flour are hard to get even at the government-controlled fair-price ration shops. Paper has become so scarce that books are prohibitively expensive. There are hardly any books to be found, even in the rooms of students, and the newspapers are referring to "the textbook famine." Aluminum is now prized almost like silver. Plastics have virtually disappeared. Residential construction has almost come to a halt, because there are grave shortages of cement, steel, wood, and glass. The price of cloth is rising so rapidly that people are buying it up in quantity. Toothpaste, soap, toilet tissue, cough mixtures, eye drops, nose drops, aspirin, antibiotics, and other toiletries and medicines have become scarce or unavailable. "Patients of epilepsy, high blood pressure, dysentery, and diarrhoea are running from chemist to chemist for drugs that are not available at any price," said a grim report in the *Times of India*.

Indians still use the British word "queue," and there are queues for practically everything. There isn't anyone, rich or poor, who is not obliged to queue for something. People have waited as long as two hours in a queue at a branch of the Punjab National Bank, only to be told that the bank had run out of money for that day. Mailing a letter may involve several queues: one for getting the letter weighed, another for buying a stamp, a third for having the stamp cancelled before one's eyes, so that it will not be used by the postal clerk to help buy a meal. Even so, there is no guarantee that the letter will ever reach its destination.

The people in the queues visibly seethe with impatience, anger, and hatred, and many a brawl breaks out, even though police are often posted to keep order. Lord Curzon, perhaps the most brilliant Englishman ever to serve as Viceroy of India, used to say that Indian rage fizzled out like soda water. Now the Indians themselves fear that the hunger, the prices, the scarcities, the endless waits, and the corruption may be turning the soda water into a Molotov cocktail.

For a year, the inflation rate has been thirty per cent. This,

combined with the chronic shortages, means hunger for millions. A representative here of the World Bank, Wolf Ladejinsky (he died in July, 1975), was often quoted in 1973 as saying, "India has twenty minutes to go to famine, and millions will die from starvation." In 1974, he was saying, "I miscalculated. I left out of account the incredible resilience of the Indian people in the face of starvation. I couldn't foresee that any Indian could survive with a meal every two days, as many Indians must have done." Among the millions of Indians who have died since Ladejinsky's original prediction, the government refuses to acknowledge that any died of starvation; it denies the existence of famine. Ever since the days of the British raj, officials here have drawn a distinction between death from starvation and death from any other cause—between faminelike conditions, which exist in some parts of the country all the time, and famine proper, which is said to exist only when deaths can be ascribed to no cause other than starvation. Such hairsplitting may have a legal function—an officially acknowledged famine entitles the disaster area to emergency government relief—but in human terms it only underlines the hopelessness of the situation.

Everyone seems to be discouraged about finding a solution to India's food problem. Large, expensive, centralized irrigation projects were completed in the nineteen-fifties and sixties, but they have turned out to be less well suited to small-farm cultivation, which is the rule in India, than had been hoped. The promise of the so-called green revolution of the late nineteen-sixties and early seventies has not been fulfilled, because the monsoon failed for two years in succession, and because there were severe shortages of electricity for irrigation pumps and of the necessary oil-based fertilizers. The government did not make a large enough investment in fertilizer plants, which are expensive and take at least four years to build, and now it cannot afford the investment, because of the quadrupling of world oil prices. "Nobody has been able to invent a cow which will give milk without being fed," writes D. P. Singh, an agricultural expert. "How can we have bumper crops if rains fail, irrigation doesn't come, electricity

is not available, and fertilizer is scarce?" Hope for any kind of genuine land reform has all but vanished, for the big landowners have become so powerful that it is widely assumed that they will always block any substantial distribution of land among the landless. They pay no income tax, and have managed to circumvent whatever legal limits there are on the size of landholdings. They finance the politicians and provide the political base of the ruling Congress Party.

India's politicians blame India's economists for the nation's economic plight. "We used to think that India had some of the world's best economists," one politican tells me. "In the sixties, they had more influence in determining economic policy here than economists had anywhere else in the world. And what a mess they made of things! We now know they are no wiser than any of the rest of us." The economists, for their part, blame self-serving, corrupt politicians, who, under India's socialist system of government, enjoy the power of licensing private businesses but use it to accumulate vast fortunes, and bungling government officials, who cannot run a single nationalized industry well—not even something as basic as the government-owned steel mills, which now work at only forty per cent of capacity. The economists say that the government has always been short on economic policy and long on socialist rhetoric. Since 1951, the government has been devising five-year plans for India's social and economic development; the draft of the fifth such plan, for the period 1974–79, is a discouraging document. A summing-up paragraph reads:

> The perspective for the next decade or so sketched out above is a modest attempt to have a measure of the task that lies ahead of us and to determine the way that we have to go. No doubt, the task is difficult and the road tortuous. But it is this that makes planning for development a perpetual adventure. It requires both vision and determination and an unshaken faith in the capacity of the country and the people to think and act big. Cynicism, inertia and fear of everything new and bold are alien to it. So are also the unwillingness to

make and demand sacrifices for a better future. Petty thought and action are as incompatible with it as wild flights of fancy and reckless deeds. Our ingrained humility has often led us to underestimate ourselves. We must discover ourselves fully. The nation is surely capable of achieving much more than the modest goals set out above. Just as there can be no movement without resistance, there can be no achievement without setbacks. The temporary difficulties must not be allowed to cloud our vision and shake our will. We have all the opportunity to create an India of our dreams. Let us seize it with both hands. A great socialist future beckons us irresistibly.

Indian economists are a cheerful, convivial lot, who see much of each other, like to talk shop, and amuse themselves by playing what amount to economic war games, constructing and tearing down theoretical models. In this activity, human problems tend to disappear. While the economists have been playing merely verbal games, the well-to-do as a class have been playing much more ominous real ones, with the result that two "parallel economies" have emerged in India: the "white economy," involving taxes, salaries, receipts, which is to say, money on the books; and the "black economy," involving bribes, unrecorded cash transactions, hidden inventories, which is to say, money off the books. There are those here who say that the black economy has outstripped the white. Instead of increasing the money on the books, the nationalization of each new industry, the rationing of each new commodity, the institution of each new control has increased the money off the books. No one here has yet been able to contain the black economy, let alone destroy it. As more and more people chase fewer and fewer necessities, who gets what—water or electricity, a telephone or a ration card—depends on whom one knows, whom one is related to, who owes one a favor, and how much one can pay. Even the democratic system seems to favor the black economy, because it provides leeway for the buying and selling of votes, of influence, and of access to the necessities of life. Arun Shourie, an Indian economist who works for the World

Bank, wrote in a recent article in the *Economic & Political Weekly,* published in Bombay:

> Ostensibly, each member of the Lok Sabha [Parliament] . . . gets elected on the premise that he has not spent more than Rs. 35,000 on his election. Similarly, the law debars each state legislator from spending more than Rs. 10,000 to 13,000. The *cognoscenti,* however, aver that an average Parliamentary election costs a candidate . . . Rs. 200,000 to Rs. 300,000 and that an average election to a state legislature costs about Rs. 100,000. When one adds expenditure on other elections—those to district bodies, co-operatives and so on—I would not be surprised if the [ruling Congress Party] alone has to muster Rs. 60–70 crores every five years. [A crore is ten million rupees, or a little over one million three hundred thousand dollars.] Many observers suggest that even this is a gross underestimate. . . . As contributions to political parties are prohibited by law, all collections are illicit. . . .
>
> Governments daily decree exceptions to announced economic policies. . . . Producers and traders are allowed to create artificial scarcities. . . . Governments never get around to strengthening the apparatus for collecting taxes and to enforcing regulations about foreign exchange.

People I meet here still dismiss the possibility of a revolution; they say that since independence the nation has not produced a single revolutionary of any stature or an ideology with any following, and that everything in Hinduism, with its rigid caste structure and its laws of karma and dharma, militates against revolution. They believe that nothing in the country will ever change—that, as always, the Indians will just go on living from crisis to crisis, and things will continue to get worse. These same people, I remember, never believed that India would be partitioned, until they woke up on August 15, 1947, and discovered that a quarter of their country had been carved out to create the state of Pakistan. Such revolutionaries as are still around are talking about a spontaneous outbreak of violence in the villages, a sort of blood-drenched food riot from one end of the country to the other—

a peasants' rebellion, sparked by, say, a major crop failure. They are equally vague about its outcome and about just what kind of government would replace the present one. For the first time, however, there is talk here of military or political dictatorship.

The main industry in New Delhi is still government. The British used to say that they educated Indians so they could have enough clerks, and, in a sense, New Delhi remains a city of clerks. There seems to be no one in authority here who can give the country leadership and direction. As a rule, Indians in positions of power think that once they have articulated a problem they have solved it, that once they have drawn up a plan they have carried it out. They're more interested in theories than in results. There are many who think that capitalism and private enterprise are bad, and therefore that it is better to do without fertilizer plants, for instance, than to have them built by private enterprise, better to forgo offshore oil exploration than to allow private companies to invest in it and profit by it.

A few years ago, people spoke of Mrs. Gandhi admiringly as "a modern mind," but now they speak of her disparagingly as "the Empress," "the Lady," "Madame," or simply "she." In 1974, when there was a threat of disruption and disorder because of a strike of railway workers, the government summarily jailed between thirty and fifty thousand of the workers, reportedly discharging a number of these and confiscating their government-owned homes; it thereby succeeded in breaking the strike and in warning workers in other government-run industries of what was in store for them if they went on strike. In drawing rooms and offices, clubs and colleges, people here have begun to question whether democracy was ever suited to Indian conditions, since the top five per cent of the people are the system's main beneficiaries; since most people must go hungry and can neither participate in the system nor enjoy its fruits; and since the population increases relentlessly every year.

Mahatma Gandhi thought that India's population growth

could be controlled by self-imposed abstinence, but the problem has proved so intractable that some foreign observers here are now questioning whether it could be controlled even by a scientific miracle like a sterilizing vaccine.

I ask an eminent population expert in the government what it is doing about population control.

"The problem is cerebral, not genital," he says. "It's psychological, not physiological. It's a matter of working out a system of rewards and punishments for childbearing couples, of offering them psychological inducements to have smaller families, like life-insurance policies for those who promise to stop at two children. You see, for the poor, children are a form of insurance."

His argument confounds me, and, taking up one of several points that occur to me, I say that we scarcely know whether a system of rewards and punishments succeeds in controlling crime, so how can we be sure that it will succeed in controlling population growth?

"The poor should not be lumped with criminals," he replies, unperturbed.

The government has been spending less than one rupee per childbearing couple per year for family planning, and it recently reduced the amount even further. I remark that such a cutback is self-defeating—that it can only mean that the government will have to allocate more money to feed more people later on.

"We'll let later on take care of itself," the expert says. "We are just concerned with getting through today. Anyway, the rate of our population growth is lower than that in many Latin-American countries, and Indians consume much less of the earth's resources per person than, say, the Westerners do. Besides, we have now entered the atomic age, and we can look forward to a day when nuclear energy will help us feed our poor. There is no reason to repeat the Western sequence of steps and move tortuously from an agrarian to an industrial to a technological to a nuclear economy. We can accelerate the process and leap all the way from an agrarian economy to a nuclear one."

The tone of all the talk here about population control is theoretical, passionless, unrealistic. It has not changed since independence. Meanwhile, the population has almost doubled.

Indians are wont to say, "It's not the government but God who gives us food. Everything depends on the monsoon." If the monsoon rains are too heavy and extensive, there are floods and devastation in the country; if they are too light and scattered, there is drought and famine. The right amount of rain for a good harvest is rare. In 1974, the monsoon rains were scanty. It had been calculated that at least a hundred and fifteen million tons of food grains would be needed to get India's six hundred million people from that monsoon to the next. The harvest was at least ten million tons short. The world's reserves of food grains are so low that India has been unable to rely on them to help her out, as she did in the past. And she has no reserves of her own.

story from Delhi which appeared on the front page of his paper under the two-column headline "Authoritarian Rule Gains Wide Acceptance in India," and in which he wrote, "In the cities and in the countryside, in the regions of the isolated rich and of the many, many poor, India is almost completely at peace, and Prime Minister Gandhi, in the opinion of knowledgeable people here, is as firmly in control as she has ever been." He went on to quote an opponent of the government who had expected a popular revolt against the Emergency as saying, "Much as I hate to admit it, the state of Emergency is popular. If the people are for it, the fact that a few chaps like me are actively against it does not make much difference." Borders then listed the following as among the reasons for the Emergency's popularity: India's problems were so unmanageable that they required a radical, nondemocratic solution; the nation's long-standing tradition of nonviolence discouraged violent revolution; and Prime Minister Gandhi's Emergency measures were succeeding to some extent in streamlining the economy—in Borders' words, "many Indians feel they are now better off, economically or in some other way, than they were before the Emergency." He reported that people from one end of the country to the other—from Calcutta to Bombay, and even in the remote villages—were praising the Emergency. The well-to-do were confident that they could now walk the city streets at night without fear. Businessmen were delighted that India was finally "getting moving." In some cases, bonded peasants were relieved by the moratoriums that had been declared upon their debts to their landlords and to moneylenders, "providing relief from a lifetime of indentured servitude on the hard, dry earth." He wrote, "The new mood is expressed this way in a recent quotation from the Prime Minister that now adorns one of the inspirational road signs that are proliferating around India: 'The only magic to remove poverty—hard work, clear vision, iron will, strictest discipline.'" As it happened, Borders was a stranger to India—he had been sent there after the Emergency—but even an old hand would have had trouble gauging the mood of six hundred million people who speak hundreds of tongues and live in an almost feudal society where the techniques of Gallup and Harris are unknown.

Foreign television was no more adept than the foreign press in getting a critical point of view on the Emergency, for Mrs. Gandhi was easily able to dominate television interviewers who, like Borders, had little or no firsthand experience of the country, and she was able to project herself on the screen as a savior of democracy and the poor. (A volume entitled "Democracy and Discipline: Speeches of Shrimati [Mrs.] Indira Gandhi" and published—a few months after the proclamation of the Emergency—by the Ministry of Information and Broadcasting, which had become the propaganda organ of the Emergency, printed a transcript of an interview she gave via satellite in August of 1975 to NBC's "Meet the Press" and also judicious excerpts from an interview she gave to North German TV.) It was difficult to gainsay propaganda, even when attacks on it by Indians in India were published abroad, such as a pseudonymous article by one Azad that appeared in August of 1976 in *The New Republic*. (Azad—the word means "free"—was revealed, during a congressional hearing on India, the following month in Washington, to be Mrs. Gandhi's first cousin Nayantara Sahgal, who was by then safely out of India, having taken up a fellowship at Harvard.) Indian journalists could no longer depend on sources at home, and they were barred from reading foreign news and comment on their country. A traveller to India in 1976 reported that at the Calcutta airport he picked up a copy of *Time* with a cover story on world torture but that when he reached Delhi, a couple of hours later, he had to get rid of the magazine, because the story contained a paragraph on torture in Mrs. Gandhi's jails and the issue had been banned. In fact, Mrs. Gandhi was prepared to go to any lengths to repress information. Not only were resident Western journalists ordered to quit the country if they happened to displease the authorities by their stories but newcomers were often denied visas or turned away at the airports, where officials were armed with the names of blacklisted journalists. (Only the West German correspondents seemed to fare better, apparently because their government tied their well-being to the continuance of German economic aid to India.) J. Anthony Lukas, the *Times'* resident correspondent from 1965 to 1967, wangled his way back into India in 1975 after the proclamation of the Emergency, and took the precaution of not publishing his impressions until he returned home. An article he wrote for the Sunday *Times Magazine,* although it was essentially bland, made one new, telling point: that Mrs. Gandhi had proclaimed the Emergency not because of the threat from the opposition, as she repeatedly asserted, but, rather, because of the threat to her power from within her own Congress Party. After the article appeared, Mrs. Gandhi's government formed an official task force to track down all Lukas's sources.

In June of 1976, following a protracted struggle with the Indian bureaucracy for a visa, Christopher Sweeney, a British journalist, went to India as a temporary correspondent for the *Guardian* and *The Economist,* neither of which was then represented there. When he had been in the country only four weeks—and had not yet filed a single line of copy—he was unceremoniously thrown out. Back in England, he reported that during those four weeks he had been constantly tailed, his mail opened, his hotel rooms broken into, his belongings rifled, and, on one occasion, the bottom of his suitcase slashed open and searched. People he talked with, he said, were harassed, critics of the government were "constantly watched, their movements reported," and, in short, "any foreign journalist, who is automatically under suspicion anyway, cannot hope to operate with any real discretion." The *Guardian* reacted to the expulsion of its correspondent in an editorial headlined "Mrs. Gandhi Locks Out the World."

In September of 1976, perhaps in reaction to criticism in the Western press, it was announced that rules for Western journalists would be relaxed, and the government subsequently went as far as to invite back representatives from expelled organizations, like the BBC, but the change was mostly illusory, since the journalists still had to work under the threat of expulsion.

Educated Indians, whether in the government, the professions, business, or the universities, have always relied mainly on gossip and hearsay for information about the government. During the Emergency, in the absence of fact, the circulation of gossip about the situation, pro and con, became institutionalized, and whenever Indians met, at home or abroad, provided they were out of range of spies and eavesdroppers, they would talk. Some of those in India took to pouring out their feelings in letters, which they entrusted to departing friends. From such talk and letters, it appeared that the Indians themselves were much more divided in their reactions to the Emergency than some Western reports had indicated.

A letter smuggled out by an Indian in New Delhi who was well placed in Mrs. Gandhi's government was dated July 7, 1975, and said:

> No doubt you would like to know how the world goes in this part of it during these history-making days. I wish to assure you with all the emphasis at my command that nothing has really changed, that the conditions here are absolutely normal, as one would expect them to be. All of us here feel that Mrs. Gandhi's strong actions on 26th *ultimo* were more than justified—they have saved the Government from being undermined by the Opposition's campaign for mass civil disobedience. Their demonstrations and strikes would only have encouraged the lawless and disorderly tendencies in our society. To give in to the Opposition, which was growing more obstreperous and destructive every day, would have been a Himalayan blunder. Mrs. Gandhi's new economic measures to control inflation and black marketeering have been welcomed, even in some Opposition quarters, and the exempting from taxation of all income under eight thousand rupees a year (a little under a thousand dollars) should be a great relief to us government servants on salaries. Previously

all income over six thousand rupees a year was taxed.

To give you some flavor of the political situation that forced Mrs. Gandhi to act, I quote below a few tidbits from the better English-language newspapers here published just before the 26th, when the press was still "free" to say anything and yet the important papers were backing Mrs. Gandhi over the Opposition. I feel sure the American press is not giving Mrs. Gandhi her due.

"The trouble with most Opposition groups here is that having never shouldered the responsibilities of office, they don't have the restraint born of an intimate knowledge of the difficulties inherent in governing a large and extremely poor country."—*The Times of India.*

" 'My eyes were set on my country. I have done no wrong for I have not done anything for myself.'—Mrs. Gandhi." —*The Sunday Statesman.*

" 'Mrs. Gandhi is a dictatorial democrat and a democratic dictator. She is woman and man as well. Woman with a masculine courage and a man with a feminine grace. She is stiff and flexible as well. Stiff in her fortitude and flexible in circumstances. . . .' From the booklet "Indira Gandhi in Her Totality" authored by a sitting Congress MP and carrying a foreword by the party President, Mr. Barooah, and a commendation by the Union Minister, Mr. Dikshit."—*The Statesman.*

A letter that was smuggled out of Calcutta nearly a year later had this to say:

A few nights ago, I listened to various overseas radio stations—BBC, Radio Australia, and Voice of America. How comforting it was to hear these voices of freedom.

Today, the 26th June, the anniversary of the Emergency, an unforgettable day for us in India, the writing on the wall is clear—Mrs. Gandhi will never restore democracy. Our censored newspapers carry reports from Samachar [the newly constituted Indian government news agency] that she thinks that though the opposition is subdued it is not yet vanquished. We have come to the conclusion that she is determined to rule this country by fear and felony, as a totalitarian dictator.

I visited Jaya Prakash Narayan [the socialist leader of the opposition] in Bombay. It was terrible to see him weak, old, and dejected. I think Death will touch his forehead one day soon. But that is not the cause of his dejection. He feels he can now do little to emancipate his people from the grip of this tyrannical witch. But still we are all working to get rid of her. To quote Benjamin Franklin, "They that can give up essential liberty to obtain a little temporary safety deserve neither liberty nor safety." There are thousands of us now working underground who would shed their last drop of blood for restoring our liberty and safety.

An Indian woman from Delhi who visited New York around the same time could not have disagreed more with this impassioned correspondent. On one occasion, she expatiated on the spread of anarchy and political chicanery before the Emergency and the imposition of law and order and political probity after it. "Things in Delhi had come to such a pass before the Emergency that hooligans would set fire to public buses," she said. "Some of them had become so bold that they would cruise around on motorcycles and snatch things from passersby in broad daylight—including a gold chain from a woman's neck—and race off. The old, faithful bearers and cooks were turning into thieves. You couldn't so much as walk around Connaught Circus without being mobbed by beggars. They had become so bold that they would catch hold of your shoes and sari, clutch at you, and set up an infernal chorus. '*Mataji* [Mother], look! My baby is dying.' '*Mataji*, I haven't had anything in my stomach for five days.' '*Mataji*, look! My arms and hands have withered away.' Your heart would go out to them, but how many could you help? What could any one person do? The poor were crawling up practically to the verandas in the best colonies and setting up their slums. The slums were completely illegal—they were on public property—but within a matter of days a politician would have a street tap and a couple of poles for electricity installed in these slums.

When I first moved into my colony, ten years ago, there were only four slums. Within those ten years, two hundred appeared.

"Hoarders and black marketeers were everywhere. They were creating artificial scarcities and inflation. I once went into a respectable shop to pick up a tin of Postman vegetable oil. The shopkeeper said he didn't have any. I pleaded with him—I'd been buying at that shop for twenty years—and he finally said, 'All right, sister, I will do you a favor. Sixty-five rupees [eight and a half dollars].' Sixty-five rupees! That was double the price of my last tin of Postman vegetable oil. But at least I had the vegetable oil. Everything was breaking down. My daughter would go to her classes at college and the professors would be out on strike. If you visited government offices, you found that the clerks and underlings had had their heads so turned by unscrupulous politicians that they were out on the lawn playing cards for all to see. Government officials never arrived at their offices on time. When you tried to ring up a public service, like the railway station or the telephone office, nobody would bother to answer, or if somebody did he was so rude and offensive that you were sorry you rang up. As for using public services, to ride a city bus was to take your life in your hands. The conductor couldn't even get around to collect the fares. People pushed and climbed their way in like vultures swooping on a still twitching corpse. Let a policeman try to discipline a hooligan or shoo away a beggar, let a government officer try to clear a slum or reprimand a clerk, let a customer lodge a complaint against a hoarder or a black marketeer, and some politician or other was sure to set up a hue and cry in Parliament about government brutality and the rights of the citizen. All that the politicians cared about was getting votes. A politician who took credit for bringing piped water and some electricity into a slum could command its votes. When the authorities dared to clear away these slums, which they did now and again, the politicians would return the next day with the slum dwellers in tow. Many politicians were not above spending money lavishly to buy votes, and their pockets were kept filled with protection money from hoarders and black marketeers. Whenever a politician had a marriage in his household, free jewels arrived. Politicians were constantly, as we say at home, thrashing their hands and feet every which way to amass wealth and power. There was no way to bring any of them to book, they were so clever—and their lawyers were cleverer still. And if these were the conditions in the capital, our showplace for foreigners, you can imagine what the rest of the country must have been like.

"And now, what calm and discipline Mrs. Gandhi has brought over the land! Everyone says that she is Goddess Durga, that she has Goddess Durga's *shakti* [energy and power] and no one can cross her without being smitten by it. She knows exactly how to act for the best effect. When she goes to a village, she wears a full-sleeved blouse and her head is demurely covered— she is dressed like a simple, God-fearing lady. When she goes to Maharashtra, she dresses like a Maharashtran, in a plain cotton sari and sandals. When she goes to Kashmir, she dresses like a Kashmiri, in pajama trousers, long shirt, and veil. But when she goes to the Soviet Union she wears a European-cut coat, her head is naked, and there are Western-type shoes on her feet. Everyone is deeply impressed by her. She has taken a whole country into her hands and has given all of us a great deal of comfort. Now there is not a hooligan or beggar to be seen anywhere in Delhi. The city looks clean, healthy, and beautiful as never before. All the slums are gone, all the beggars are gone, and so are all the riffraff of hawkers from Connaught Circus. They've all been swept away. Even the tent in the street where students, laborers, and other rabble-rousers would congregate and drink coffee has been pulled down, and a low-priced, modern coffeehouse has been established in a building. The beggars, slum dwellers, and hawkers now live in new satellite developments on the outskirts of the city, and Mrs. Gandhi buses them in for an honest day's work in the morning and buses them out at night. My sweeper and my washerwoman, who both used to live in my colony slum, come in on buses now.

"Mrs. Gandhi has devised all kinds of ways to catch hoarders and black marketeers. Anyone, young or old, who helps to catch one of them gets a percentage of whatever is found. Just the other day, we were shown on television a beautiful temple with a beautiful statue of Lord Krishna. Behind it, buried in the ground and wall, were money and jewelry. The information was given by the mason who had built the hollow back wall. The mason got a share for giving information against the rich profiteer. As a consequence of this vigilance, all the prices have come down. The hoarded foodstuffs have been delivered to the markets. The tins of vegetable oil are now in the front of the shops, properly marked. I bought a tin of Postman vegetable oil just the other day for thirty-two rupees. Whenever Mrs. Gandhi loosens her grip even slightly, though, the prices tend to go up. Everything works now. Classes in universities meet regularly, and examinations are held on the appointed days; buses and trains run on time. Mrs. Gandhi has given an order that every government employee must arrive on time and not leave his office until it's time to go. This applies to all officers, high or low, all members of the staff. Everyone in public service picks up the telephone immediately and greets you politely with a sweet tongue, in a disciplined way. Conductors are posted at bus stops, and no one can get on the bus without a ticket, and practically everyone who has a ticket can find a seat. If anyone tries to rush past the conductor, the conductor immediately summons a policeman and gets the miscreant booked. The people who used to sneak onto buses and trains are in jail. No matter what riches and power you have, they do you no good. You can't use them to hire a lawyer and stay out of jail. The truth is that we Indians are by nature thieves, black marketeers, and cheats. We have a very bad character. The British knew that the only way to rule us was with a stick. Mrs. Gandhi understands that and has now taken hold of that stick. She is very clever. She has even managed to control the youth. She gives audiences to children and students regularly. She makes them all sit down around her and ask her questions. She answers all their questions and imbues them with the spirit of nationalism, national pride, and national discipline. She says things like 'Now you have to make this nation. You have to take the work of building this nation onto your shoulders.' And when children all across the country read these remarks, they feel thrilled and inspired.''

# 2

# Democracy in a
# Poor Country

Aristotle, in his "Politics," laid down the prerequisites for a good form of democratic government, the most basic being that the majority of the people should belong to the middle class and have an economic stake in their society—should, for instance, own property:

> The city which is composed of middle-class citizens is necessarily best governed; they are, as we say, the natural elements of a state. And this is the class of citizens which is most secure in a state, for they do not, like the poor, covet their neighbors' goods; nor do others covet theirs, as the poor covet the goods of the rich; and as they neither plot against others, nor are themselves plotted against, they pass through life safely. Wisely then did Phocylides pray—
>
> "Many things are best in the mean; I desire to be of a middle condition in my city."
>
> Thus it is manifest that the best political community is formed by citizens of the middle class, and that those states are likely to be well-administered, in which the middle class is large, and larger if possible than both the other classes, or at any rate than either singly; for the addition of the middle class turns the scale, and prevents either of the extremes from being dominant. Great then is the good fortune of a state in

which the citizens have a moderate and sufficient property; for where some possess much, and the others nothing, there may arise an extreme democracy [in his terms a form of anarchy], or a pure oligarchy; or a tyranny may grow out of either extreme—either out of the most rampant democracy, or out of an oligarchy; but it is not so likely to arise out of a middle and nearly equal condition. (*Benjamin Jowett's translation.*)

That this was the most basic prerequisite became a firmly held belief among classical political thinkers, and it helped to inspire the democratic institutions of such preponderantly middle-class nations as Great Britain, France, and the United States. In 1947, however, independent India, flying in the face of this philosophical tradition—and, indeed, of its own long history of oligarchy—dared to set up a democratic form of government consciously modelled on that of Great Britain and the United States, and thus began what its first Prime Minister, Jawaharlal Nehru, along with his Western admirers, liked to call an "adventure in democracy." People who had never learned to sign their names and who were so backward that in some cases they had scarcely heard of the wheel or the nail would journey by yak or on foot for several days to vote by secret ballot in ballot boxes that they could identify only by means of party ideographs. To insure that everyone who wanted to vote could vote, the government went to such lengths that general elections sometimes took as much as three months to complete. However inefficient and imperfect the system was, it helped to keep the country united by allowing political expression to India's diverse races, regions, religions, castes, cultures, and languages. The people elected to the Parliament and to the state legislatures were as diverse as the people they represented. They wore everything from Savile Row suits to tribal dress, and spoke in Oxford accents or in languages known only in remote villages. The people and their representatives all paid homage to Nehru, whose self-restraint, patriotism, and lifelong devotion to British socialist ideas of democracy had made the "adventure" possible in the first place.

Before the establishment of the democracy, Nehru had led
India in the fight for freedom for a quarter of a century, and he
understood how easy it would be for someone as wellborn and
well off as he was to bask in the adulation of the poor and the
illiterate and to arrogate to himself extraordinary powers in the
deluded belief that he alone knew what was best for his people.
He had come to political maturity at the time of the rise of Fascism
and was familiar with the lures and arguments of Fascist dictators.
He was always on his guard in case he should end up as one of
them. As early as 1937, he published anonymously, in a Calcutta
periodical called *Modern Review,* an article about himself as a
would-be dictator. His daughter and only child, Indira, was apparently one of the few people who knew the identity of the
author until, some four years later, Nehru disclosed his "trick"
in an autobiography, "Toward Freedom." The article reads, in
part:

> "Rashtrapati Jawaharlal ki Jai!" [Nehru was repeating a
> popular cheer, "All hail Jawaharlal, father of the nation!"]
> The Rashtrapati looked up as he passed swiftly through the
> waiting crowds, his hands went up and were joined together
> in salute and his pale hard face was lit up by a smile. It was
> a warm personal smile and the people who saw it responded
> to it immediately and smiled and cheered in return.
> The smile passed away and again the face became stern and
> sad, impassive in the midst of the emotion that it had roused
> in the multitude. Almost it seemed that the smile and the
> gesture accompanying it had little reality behind them; they
> were just tricks of the trade to gain the good-will of the
> crowds whose darling he had become. Was it so? . . .
> From the far North to Cape Comorin he has gone like
> some triumphant Caesar passing by, leaving a trail of glory
> and a legend behind him. Is all this for him just a passing
> fancy which amuses him, or some deep design or the play of
> some force which he himself does not know? Is it his will to
> power . . . that is driving him from crowd to crowd and
> making him whisper to himself:

I drew these tides of men into my hands
and wrote my will across the sky in stars.

What if the fancy turn? Men like Jawaharlal with all their capacity for great and good work are unsafe in democracy. He calls himself a democrat and a socialist, and no doubt he does so in all earnestness, but every psychologist knows that the mind is ultimately a slave to the heart and that logic can always be made to fit in with the desires and irrepressible urges of man. A little twist and Jawaharlal might turn a dictator, sweeping aside the paraphernalia of a slow-moving democracy. He might still use the language and slogans of democracy and socialism, but we all know how fascism has fattened on this language and then cast it away as useless lumber. . . .

Jawaharlal cannot become a fascist. And yet he has all the makings of a dictator in him—vast popularity, a strong will directed to a well-defined purpose, energy, pride, organizational capacity, ability, hardness, and, with all his love of the crowd, an intolerance of others and a certain contempt for the weak and inefficient. His flashes of temper are well-known and even when they are controlled, the curling of the lips betrays him. His overmastering desire to get things done, to sweep away what he dislikes and build anew, will hardly brook for long the slow processes of democracy. He may keep the husk but he will see to it that it bends to his will. In normal times he would just be an efficient and successful executive, but in this revolutionary epoch Caesarism is always at the door, and is it not possible that Jawaharlal might fancy himself as a Caesar?

Therein lies danger for Jawaharlal and for India. For it is not through Caesarism that India will attain freedom, and though she may prosper a little under a benevolent and efficient despotism, she will remain stunted and the day of the emancipation of her people will be delayed.

Nehru served as free India's Prime Minister for almost seventeen years. In retrospect, one can criticize him for forfeiting the chance that his national popularity gave him to truly revolutionize the social and economic relationships among castes and classes, and so to attack the roots of poverty. But he was, for the most part, scrupulous in preserving the spirit of the "adventure." He did not appoint his daughter, for instance, to any high government post or encourage her to acquire any personal power. There is no clear evidence that he planned for her to inherit his office one day. He could probably have named any successor he liked, but he made sure that after his death democratic procedures would be observed in the election of the next Prime Minister.

Lal Bahadur Shastri succeeded Nehru as Prime Minister, and, partly to honor Nehru's memory, appointed Indira Gandhi his Minister of Information and Broadcasting—a relatively secondary portfolio. Shastri died prematurely in 1966, after serving for less than two years, and left India again with the problem of succession. In the Congress Party, there were several strong contenders for the office; each had long political experience and a loyal following, but each aroused deep hostility in the camps of the other contenders. The Party bosses—popularly called the Syndicate—eventually backed Mrs. Gandhi, and she won. She was thought to be innocuous and inexperienced, and, being known primarily as a woman of good breeding, was expected to be a decorative figurehead. Indeed, in her early days in office she was looked upon as a puppet Prime Minister, with the Syndicate pulling the strings. In a crisis, she would display extreme docility and make her cause that of whichever faction in the Party had the blessing of the Syndicate and so commanded the most power. Before long, however, it became apparent that she had a mind of her own, and was quite capable of abandoning the course of action advocated by the Syndicate and pushing her own ideas whenever she saw an opportunity to rally members of the Party around her. Surprise at Mrs. Gandhi's revelations of strength, restiveness among the younger Congress members who had been under the thumb of the Syndicate, and the power and patronage of the office of the Prime Minister all worked in her favor. Moreover, she presented herself as a socialist and a democrat, like her father—a "modern mind," with progressive ideas, whose realization was constantly frustrated by the backward-looking, self-seeking Syndicate. In 1969, she gave dramatic evidence of her ability to beat the Syndicate members at their own game. They had made a strong bid to install one of their own number, Sanjiva Reddy, as the President of India. The President, who is the titular head of the government and commander-in-chief of the armed forces, is elected by the members of Parliament and of the state assemblies. Mrs. Gandhi reluctantly supported the Syndicate's candidate for a time, and then decided to support a candidate of her own, V. V. Giri. Giri won, and the power of the Syndicate was never the same again.

Mrs. Gandhi, however, still had to win at the polls. To do so, she was obliged to depend on the same power base and the same narrow constituency as the Syndicate—namely, the Congress Party and the small middle class it actually represented. Yet if she ever really hoped to put into effect her often proclaimed progressive socialist reforms—for example, genuine land redistribution for the poor—she could do so only at the expense of her party and that class, and if she ran afoul of them she stood to lose the power and office she needed to effect those reforms. This was her dilemma. Her father, too, though he had been able to appeal to a certain amount of idealism in the Party and the middle class, had been defeated by that dilemma in his efforts to make significant social and economic progress. In the end, apparently, for both father and daughter staying in office took precedence over reform. Mrs. Gandhi soon proved adept at winning elections. She portrayed herself as the leader who could best carry on her father's unfinished work; she inundated the country with slogans like "*Gharibi hatao*" ("Abolish poverty"); and, thanks in part to some stunning military successes against Pakistan in the 1971 war that led to the creation of Bangladesh, she came to be known at home and abroad for her "realism" and "realpolitik."

In 1971, however, Mrs. Gandhi became involved in a much publicized court case arising out of that year's general elections. She had stood as a Congress candidate for Parliament in the Rae Bareli constituency, in her home state of Uttar Pradesh, and had beaten her opponent, a Socialist Party candidate named Raj Narain, by a large margin. Immediately after her victory, Narain charged her with fourteen violations of the 1951 electoral law, and carried the case to the state's high court, in Allahabad. For a long time, no one took the matter seriously. After all, Mrs. Gandhi was the Prime Minister, and her family had wielded considerable power and influence in Allahabad for many generations, whereas Narain was a minor country politician. But he persisted. The case dragged on, and eventually, in 1975, Mrs. Gandhi reluctantly testified in her own defense. She was on the stand for seven and a half hours. On June 12th of that year, a judgment was finally handed down, and Mrs. Gandhi was found guilty of two of the fourteen charges. One concerned her use of an official from her secretariat, Yashpal Kapoor, in her election campaign for a brief period while he was still on the government's payroll. The other concerned her use of local officials to set up rostrums and loudspeakers for two political rallies. The electoral law prescribed severe penalties for anyone convicted of such "corrupt practices." Mrs. Gandhi was sentenced to give up her seat in Parliament and to hold no elective office for six years. She immediately appealed to the Supreme Court, in New Delhi.

On the face of it, both violations were trivial, especially since, as Prime Minister, Mrs. Gandhi legally had the whole paraphernalia of government at her disposal at election time; for instance, she used government helicopters as a matter of course to fly from rally to rally. But the opposition parties, which had never governed the country, immediately seized on her conviction as proof of corruption in every part of the central government—of the corruption of the people in office and the virtuousness of the people out of office. They clamored for her resignation, dramatizing the issue of corruption to win popular support.

India's short experience with democratic government had been permeated by corruption. The demands on the country's resources were so overwhelming that opportunities for corruption were rife. With huge numbers of the poor living on a narrow margin of survival, enormous prizes were available to members of the middle class as hoarders, speculators, black marketeers, and smugglers. In theory, government officials and elected representatives were supposed to serve everybody, but in practice they were beholden only to the class they came from, so while they were vociferous in their condemnation of corruption, little was done about it. Hence, the gap between the democratic system of law and the devices of self-serving politics, between the expression of noble intentions and sentiments and the resort to base performance and tactics, widened all the time. Stringent legal penalties for corruption were often enacted to assuage sensitive consciences but were rarely enforced. Mrs. Gandhi's conviction was a spectacular exception, and it came at a particularly difficult moment for her, when opposition to her government was crystallizing around Jaya Prakash Narayan and Morarji Desai.

Both Narayan and Desai were national figures, stalwarts of the freedom struggle and veterans of the Congress Party, although Narayan had become a staunch socialist and Desai a conservative. In contrast to Nehru and Mrs. Gandhi, Narayan had abandoned the Congress Party in 1948 and the entire middle-class power base some six years later to seek social and economic reform outside the regular channels of politics, and he had been wandering through India's villages preaching spiritual socialism. In March, 1974, however, he became the center of an essentially middle-class protest movement of students, workers, and intellectuals in his native Bihar, one of the poorest states in India. The movement advocated a "partyless democracy" through "total revolution," which would employ political agitation—sit-ins, strikes, boycotts—to rid the state and the country of corrupt, inefficient governments. But Narayan and his crusaders had no clearer idea than the Congress Party about how reform was to be effected and the middle class made to share power and wealth with the poor. Their crusade mainly took the form of moral exhortations and long processions—often silent, to emphasize the nonviolent character of Narayan's "revolution."

In the meantime, Desai was sponsoring another protest movement, in Gujarat, his home state. Unlike Narayan, Desai, a tough, pugnacious man, was a politician in the traditional mold. He had served as Minister of Finance in Nehru's government and had been Mrs. Gandhi's main rival for the office of Prime Minister. Afterward, he had served as Minister of Finance and Deputy Prime Minister in her government until 1969, when she ousted him. The Gujarat state government had been in turmoil for some years. Opposition parties had overthrown its Congress majority through political agitation, forced a new election, formed a coalition with the Congress, and then overthrown the state government again. Mrs. Gandhi had started governing the state from Delhi by proclamation, under an emergency provision of the constitution known as President's Rule. The opposition parties had condemned the imposition of President's Rule as corrupt and anti-democratic and had begun agitating for a new election, which it was generally expected would put them in power. In April, 1975, to force the issue, Desai undertook a fast "unto death." Mrs. Gandhi, fearful of the political consequences of his death, gave in. Narayan and Desai now made an alliance of convenience and, out of half a dozen small, disparate parties, formed a so-called People's Front for the purpose of winning the Gujarat election. As a political party, the People's Front was probably better suited to nonviolent protest and political agitation than to forming a government, yet it had an enormous psychological effect on the Congress Party. The messianic Narayan and the aggressive Desai were laying claim to a political power base of their own.

Since 1971, opposition to the Congress Party had been growing throughout the country. The very costly war with Pakistan that year had left a legacy of high inflation, and this was compounded by drought and famine in several subsequent years and, in 1974, by the fourfold increase in the world price of oil, vital for India's chemical-fertilizer industry and the green revolution. Those national afflictions were further exacerbated by constant student and worker strikes, the government's economic mismanagement, and political corruption, and Mrs. Gandhi's slogans began to ring hollow. President's Rule was imposed on several states in the name of law and order, even as Galbraith's description of India as a "functioning anarchy" became more and more apt. In these states and elsewhere, opposition parties more extremist than Narayan's and Desai's, having been denied the opportunity to fight elections, grew more and more vociferous and in some cases took to violence. On the right, there was the increasingly powerful Jana Sangh, a Hindu chauvinist party with a paramilitary organization and strong nationalist backing, which appealed to narrow social and religious prejudices. The left, though ideologically split, had also been gaining ground, thanks to the appearance, in 1967, of the Naxalites, a Maoist peasant movement that originated in a district of West Bengal called Naxalbari. Its violent ideology, its genuine peasant roots, and the revolutionary example of neighboring China had attracted to it many middle-class idealists and malcontents, students and intellectuals, and it had quickly spread from Naxalbari to Calcutta and from Calcutta to Bihar and other states. It had been largely checked in the early seventies by perhaps the most ruthless government action ever taken in democratic India, when, according to unofficial reports, thousands of suspected Naxalites were liquidated under the personal orders of Mrs. Gandhi. But the memory of the Naxalites continued to inspire the left. In any event, the Congress Party seemed to be losing its automatic national support —the heritage of its role in the freedom struggle—as the general elections set for February, 1976, drew nearer. Political rhetoric everywhere was stepped up. Opposition leaders repeatedly charged the Congress with Fascism, and the Congress charged the opposition with loosing anarchy.

Then, on June 12, 1975, came Mrs. Gandhi's conviction, and, the following day, the results of the Gujarat elections, which the Narayan-Desai alliance won by a significant margin. Narayan and Desai, encouraged by their success, instituted a series of "Resign, Indira" rallies in Delhi. The Congress Party began holding counter-rallies calling for law and order. On June 24th, Mrs. Gandhi received a conditional stay of her sentence from the Supreme Court: she was allowed to remain provisionally as Prime Minister, but not as a paid or voting member of Parliament. On June 25th, at a mass rally in Delhi, Narayan announced a week-long campaign of demonstrations and civil disobedience throughout the country, beginning June 29th, to force Mrs. Gandhi's resignation. In the course of his speech, he denounced her continuance in office as illegal and unconstitutional, and exhorted the police and the military to disobey government orders repugnant to their consciences. He had made such exhortations in earlier speeches, but now, in the context of the resignation drive, the Congress interpreted the exhortations as a call for mutiny. Or so it claimed. That night, the police arrested Narayan, Desai, and leaders of all the other opposition parties (the pro-Soviet Communist Party, which had consistently supported Mrs. Gandhi, because of her government's pro-Soviet policies, was left alone), along with a number of dissident Congress Party leaders. On June 26th, the government, invoking the emergency provision of the constitution, proclaimed a state of emergency in the entire country. Because the action was so swift, the blackout on newspapers so thorough, and government propaganda about the threat to India's internal security so relentless, it was many days, even weeks, before much of the newspaper-reading public became aware of the extent of the coup; some of the hundreds of millions of poor who live in the villages of India may not have heard of it for a year or more. The mass support for the opposition parties, so much in evidence during the protest demonstrations and processions, simply melted away—a confirmation of the fact that the conflict between the Congress and those parties was in essence just a quarrel among middle-class politicians.

With the exception of twenty-eight years of democratic government, and perhaps some of the more halcyon days of the British raj, India over the centuries had known little but despotism, at the hands of native, Mogul, Portuguese, Dutch, and French rulers. It had no tradition of parliamentary democracy, of general elections, of civil liberties. Even the tradition of "maintaining law and order" and the independent judiciary to insure it were not indigenous; before the British raj was established, in 1858, anarchy and despotism had been pervasive. In fact, the most abiding tradition was that of an authoritarian, arbitrary government, personified as Ma-Bap (or Mother-Father), but Ma-Bap was more feared than loved, more remote and awesome than personal and indulgent; the only experience that most subjects had of Ma-Bap was in terms of persecutions, exactions, and confiscations.

With some justification, critics denounced the Indian democracy from its inception as an "irrelevant encumbrance," often having more to do with bread and circuses than with good government, since most of India's people were so poor that they had to be concerned primarily about having food in their stomachs rather than about enjoying their civil liberties; as a "bourgeois democracy," whose main beneficiaries were the few well-to-do; as an "alien institution," which only thinly masked an essentially rigid, caste-ridden society; as a "constitutional pipe dream," which existed solely on paper; as a "fraud," perpetuated by the worst political corruption the world had ever seen; as a "tissue of lies," which would not survive the test of history. Nevertheless, for almost twenty-eight years that Indian democracy succeeded in providing necessary, if fragile, restraints on the exercise of naked power. And in a country in which the majority of the people are utterly destitute and helpless the most important function of government may well be to provide such restraints—to protect its people from unrestricted harassment and exploitation. Self-restraint, discipline, and high-mindedness in political life were among Mahatma Gandhi's greatest legacies, and because Indian leaders coming after him had his inspiring example to guide them, they showed such restraint in the exercise of their power that Indian democracy, over more than a quarter of a century, was indeed a miracle. Then, however, within a matter of days, Mrs. Gandhi abandoned the self-restraint she had previously shown, and so, in one stroke, put in jeopardy whatever restraints had taken root in Indian democracy. Since there were no entrenched democratic traditions and institutions in India, she was able to carry out her coup with alarming ease. Her impulse may have been selfish—to stay in office at all costs; arrogant—stemming from a belief that she alone could lead India; calculating—to gain some time for coping with her political woes; panicky—to quickly immobilize the opposition for fear it would overtake her; cynical—to capitalize on the weaknesses of Indian democracy; narcissistic—to identify her destiny with India's; or disinterested, as she claimed—to save Indian democracy from its enemies. Whatever the impulse, in acting upon it she was threatening to destroy for good those delicate restraints on the exercise of naked power which had effectively kept all the enemies of Indian democracy, from Hindu Fascists to Maoist Marxists, at bay. By her Emergency, she risked making it possible for politicians, much more ruthless and power-hungry than she, one day to dislodge her and perpetrate abuses of power previously unimagined. She might have locked up her opposition, but she might also have released a political weapon every bit as potent and destructive as the atomic "device" that her government successfully exploded in May of 1974. Her greatest legacy to independent India, it appeared, was to be this newer and more subtle weapon.

# 3

# Constitutional Dictatorship

When Mrs. Gandhi received the news of her Allahabad conviction and the Gujarat defeat, she was already reeling from a loss of support in the Parliament by members of her own party. The Congress Party held three hundred and sixty-one of a total of five hundred and twenty seats. On the left, fifty or sixty Congress members who were in sympathy with Narayan's movement—the so-called Young Turks—had ganged up against her, and on the right, sixty or seventy Congress members who were not in sympathy with her professed socialist goals were agitating to replace her with their leader; he was Jagjivan Ram, Mrs. Gandhi's Minister of Irrigation and Agriculture, who had risen from the ranks of some hundred million Untouchables, among whom he had powerful support. The preëminent position of her party had never before come under such strong challenge, and not since 1969, when she joined battle with the Syndicate and the Congress old guard and vanquished it, had her hold on the Party been so tenuous. She had appealed her conviction to the Supreme Court, and Lukas reported that while she waited for a decision on the appeal she considered temporarily relinquishing the office of Prime Minister to one of several trusted advisers: Swaran Singh, the Minister of Defense at the time; Siddhartha Ray, the chief minister of West Bengal; or D. K. Barooah, the president of the Congress Party. The strategy had much to recommend it. She would diffuse the focus of the opposition protest movement and so, to some extent, discredit it. She would win popular personal support, since she would be seen as a martyr to an unjust opposition campaign to hound her from office. She would appear as an ordinary citizen attending to her case, which she was almost certain of winning. Some jurists already held that she might have violated the letter of the electoral law but had not violated its spirit. In any event, the Supreme Court was essentially hers, and the Chief Justice, A. N. Ray, was her man; he had been appointed over the heads of three other senior Supreme Court justices, almost causing a rebellion in the profession. Her strategy had one flaw, which her advisers were quick to point out: once she relinquished the office of Prime Minister, however temporarily, Jagjivan Ram was certain to engineer a coup against her stand-in and become Prime Minister himself—he had both the personal ambition and the necessary clout in the Party—and if he did she would not be able to dislodge him, whatever the decision of the Supreme Court. It was apparently at this juncture, Lukas and others reported, that Mrs. Gandhi received a piece of advice from an unexpected quarter—from Sanjay Gandhi, her younger son. (Her elder son, Rajiv, who is a pilot, has shown no consistent interest in politics.) Sanjay, then a twenty-eight-year-old car mechanic, who had been trying for the previous five years to build a huge automobile-assembly plant for the manufacture of his Maruti, had from the outset been the target of relentless attacks from the press and the Parliament, from the opposition, and from some Congress members, who charged him with corruption and mismanagement—the kind of charges that were now being levelled at Mrs. Gandhi and her government. Sanjay advised his mother to take all power into her hands and, according to Lukas, teach one and all "a lesson they'll never forget."

Sanjay's remedy was both simple and constitutional. Under the emergency provisions of the constitution, the Prime Minister could inform the President that a grave internal or external threat to the country existed, and direct him to proclaim a national emergency, which, in effect, would suspend the constitution and the normal political processes, conferring extraordinary powers on the government for the duration of the emergency. Moreover, Sanjay's remedy, like Sanjay's car, had a distinctively Indian quality. Down through the ages, India had known not only despots but also enlightened, benevolent monarchs and emperors, and these had been revered as great lawgivers and friends of the poor. For some time, Mrs. Gandhi and various other Congress leaders had been sounding the theme that India's parliamentary democracy was a Western transplant, better suited to the needs of the affluent nations; they had been saying that the constitutional guarantees of individual rights, of elections, of freedom of assembly and association, of judicial review, and even of the right to own property were blocking reform. The political turmoil leading up to Mrs. Gandhi's conviction and the Gujarat defeat was seen as the final piece of evidence that the transplanted Western institutions had in fact broken down.

All the same, Mrs. Gandhi hesitated for days before deciding on the Emergency. Her father and Mahatma Gandhi had been the twin founders of that parliamentary democracy. Although she may have felt she would be acting from the noblest of impulses, to help the poor and save the country from grave internal threat, the fact that she and her party would benefit would leave both open to charges of a self-serving coup, even if the emergency was presented as temporary and as necessary bitter medicine. Mrs. Gandhi did nothing until the evening of June 25th. Then she was told about the large "Resign, Indira" rally in Delhi, at which Jaya Prakash Narayan had called on soldiers and police not to obey government orders repugnant to their consciences. She construed this as nothing less than a call to the instruments of law and order to mutiny. Any objective person, she felt, could see that in instituting an emergency she would now only be acting in the national interest and saving the integrity and unity of the country.

On her recommendation, the late President Fakhruddin Ali Ahmed, who owed his nomination for the office to her, and who was known as an old Party henchman, signed the emergency proclamation that evening, and it was put into effect in the early hours of the next morning.

Beginning June 26th, Mrs. Gandhi governed India under the emergency provisions set out in Article 352 of the constitution. The Constituent Assembly, which drafted the constitution of democratic India in 1949, had been dominated by middle-class intellectuals. At the time, one of them, H. V. Kamath, had voiced fears about the emergency laws which later seemed prophetic: "I have studied the major constitutions of the world, but I have not come across any such wide and sweeping provision. I fear that we are seeking to lay the foundations of a totalitarian state. The suspension of fundamental rights is a very grave matter. I will go so far as to say that it is even graver than the gravest emergency with which the state may be confronted." The laws had nonetheless been written into the constitution, mainly on the ground that India was so big, so diverse, and so poor, with such a long history of internal wars and foreign conquests, that the government had to be armed with extraordinary powers if the nation was to survive at all.

The idea and the rationale for a national emergency were taken directly from the British colonial rulers, who regularly proclaimed such a condition in the name of "law and order" and made use of the so-called Defense of India Rules to peremptorily arrest political opponents of their government. And since independence the Indian government had proclaimed several national emergencies, during wars with China and with Pakistan. Each time, the government had cited an external threat to the country and presented the state of emergency as a "quick fix" for a national crisis, but the emergency had only enhanced the atmosphere of crisis, and, indeed, the external emergency proclaimed at the outbreak of the Bangladesh war, in 1971, was still in effect when the new, internal emergency was proclaimed. But the new emergency had no precedent in scope and severity. Mrs. Gandhi claimed that the opposition, the press, the courts—indeed, the constitution itself—had retarded social and economic progress; all these institutions, she said, were forces for reaction, which, interacting with vested caste and class interests, had obstructed the realization of social and economic democracy. All constitutional constraints on the use of arbitrary power were thus presented as evil, and the use of arbitrary power as a force for good.

The Prime Minister now summarily arrested her opponents—numbering in the tens of thousands, and including members of Parliament and of various state legislatures. To have arrested Jaya Prakash Narayan was almost as if she had arrested her own father. To have arrested Morarji Desai was almost as if she were trying to overturn the verdict at the polls in Gujarat. She quickly also arrested Raj Narain, and, since her conviction was under appeal, for her to arrest him was almost as if Richard Nixon, in the waning days of his Presidency, had arrested John Doar. The comparison between Mrs. Gandhi and Richard Nixon is by no means farfetched. In a speech over All-India Radio justifying her action, Mrs. Gandhi announced that she had had the arrests made for the sake of preserving law and order, and that by destroying democracy temporarily she might in fact be saving it, and she said at one point, "It is not important whether I remain Prime Minister or not. However, the institution of the Prime Minister is important"—words reminiscent of Nixon's repeated insistence that what he was trying to protect was not himself but the Presidency. In the manner of Nixon, Mrs. Gandhi, ever since taking office, had evidently fancied herself to be a pragmatist and a realist, who knew how to make tough decisions and knew what was best for the country. In recent years, the advisers around her, who were sometimes called "the Kashmiri Mafia," had been full of talk about "image," about the "realities of power," and about Mrs. Gandhi's "diplomatic triumphs."

Only a few weeks after the proclamation of the Emergency, Mrs. Gandhi set about making Parliament amend the constitution to strengthen the executive at the expense of the courts and of the Parliament itself. Her first amendment barred judicial challenges to the government's rationale for proclaiming an emergency. Another barred judicial review of the results of any election involving, among others, the Prime Minister, and retroactively rendered "pending proceedings in respect of such election under the existing law null and void." It also granted Prime Ministers immunity from criminal and civil proceedings for offenses committed before they assumed office and while they held office. Mrs. Gandhi was able to push these amendments through with a semblance of legitimacy because her party enjoyed an unprecedented two-thirds majority not only in the Parliament but in twenty of the twenty-two state legislatures, two-thirds of which were required to ratify them.

As time went on, the amendments were buttressed by a series of extraordinary laws and ordinances (one, besides dealing with more general matters, nullified retroactively the specific charges on which Mrs. Gandhi was found guilty of corrupt election practices) insuring that if Mrs. Gandhi should direct the President of India to call off the Emergency, the fundamental changes it had ushered in would continue. In the light of the constitutional and legislative changes, the Supreme Court, with Ray as Chief Justice, quickly overturned Mrs. Gandhi's conviction, without addressing itself to the question of whether the government had the right to amend the constitution in such a way as to change its fundamental nature.

Next, Mrs. Gandhi moved against the press, issuing several ordinances. One repealed a 1956 law that granted immunity to journalists reporting on Parliamentary debates—a law that, ironically, had been sponsored by Mrs. Gandhi's late husband, Feroze Gandhi. Another ordinance abolished the Press Council, an independent watchdog committee of journalists. A third was the ban on "publication of objectionable matter." (The government had always controlled radio and television directly, and, to some extent, newspapers indirectly, through the allocation of newsprint and other supplies.) Meanwhile, a set of rigid press guidelines ordered the press to dwell on the achievements of the country instead of harping on its shortcomings. (The newspapers were soon filled with stories like one about a war on rats in Delhi; with long exhortations by Mrs. Gandhi; and with accounts of speeches by Cabinet Ministers and of opening ceremonies conducted by Deputy Ministers and Departmental Secretaries.) Mrs. Gandhi accompanied these ordinances and press guidelines with a drive to capture control of the leading newspapers. Since in many cases the newspaper owners were big industrialists who depended on the government for licenses and supplies, they were hardly in a position to resist. The government got the owners of the *Indian Express,* the national English-language daily with the largest circulation, to agree "voluntarily" that six of the eleven members of its board of directors, including its chairman, would now be appointed by the government, and that its editor-in-chief, S. Mulgaonkar, would be peremptorily retired in favor of V. K. Narasimhan. Other veteran editors and journalists were similarly silenced. When *Opinion,* a four-page English-language weekly with a circulation of a few thousand, was ordered closed down by the government, its editor put out one more issue, in which he wrote:

Dear Reader,

This is to explain why there will be no more issues of *Opinion*. . . . What a tribute . . . these mighty, powerful Governments pay to *Opinion* readership and *Opinion* when they decide that they cannot allow this tiny organ of public information and public reasoning to live! . . . The current Indira regime, founded on June 26, 1975, was born through lies, nurtured by lies, and flourishes by lies. The essential ingredient of its being is the lie. Consequently, to have a truth-loving, straight-thinking, plain-speaking journal examine it week after week and point out its falsehoods becomes intolerable to it. The feeling grows, this is too much, this just can't be endured, why, it might even affect the dictatorship. . . .

In such periods it is important to realize that the seat of freedom in man is the mind. Preserve its integrity and all is not lost. The pressures upon a man may be enormous, yet if he sees clearly and judges accordingly, there is still room for hope. . . . And so, farewell.

The government stationed censors in Delhi and in all the state capitals, to censor not only news stories and advertisements in newspapers and magazines but also books, plays, and films. Although radio and television daily churned out propaganda for Mrs. Gandhi and her party, the government combined the country's two main independent syndicated news agencies, the Press Trust of India and the United News of India, into Samachar, which started feeding a steady diet of good news—the unveiling of yet another new plan to eradicate poverty, for instance—to eight hundred and thirty newspapers, published in some twenty languages. But controlling the news at its source, in the manner of Tass, was not enough. The government instructed newspapers and magazines not only what to print in each issue but also, specifically, what not to print; for example, any story about or comment on transfers of judges for handing down decisions unfavorable to the government (a ploy to curb and break judicial independence), any report on a rise in prices, any news of a hunger strike threatened by Vinoba Bhave to protest cow slaughter, any laudatory comment on the Israelis' Entebbe raid. One order forbade papers to report that a prominent Indian actress had been arrested for shoplifting in London; apparently, the story was thought bad for India's new image. Despite all this, a pamphlet brought out by the Ministry of Information and Broadcasting claimed that during the Emergency it had never interfered with the content of the news, only improved its quantity and quality. "While the government authority in India keeps itself scrupulously away from the functioning of the press," the pamphlet stated, "the initiative taken by it has considerably helped the growth of the press spatially and in depth. The press in India has been the beneficiary of several official measures, and its freedom of operation has been singularly free from any type of interference."

In July of 1976, the government played host to a gathering called the Ministerial Conference of Non-Aligned Countries on the Press Agencies Pool. The announced purpose of the event was to encourage non-aligned countries to exchange news about each other through official indigenous news agencies, like Samachar, instead of relying on the "biassed," "colonial," and "imperialistic" Western news agencies—United Press International, the Associated Press, and Reuters. In inaugurating the conference, Mrs. Gandhi said:

> Rather than unguardedly accepting versions put out by news agencies and publishing houses of the Western countries, we should get to know one another directly and keep in touch to have first-hand acquaintance with our respective views. . . . The Western media interpreted [the Emergency] as an onslaught on democracy or an abrogation of our constitution, which was not at all correct. Most, if not all, developing countries understood the position. Yet many were misled into believing the Western versions to be objective reporting. When something false is said about us we can know what is true and what is untrue. But when there is a false report about others, we cannot immediately discern its veracity or otherwise. You must have heard the old saying: "Doctors bury their mistakes. Lawyers hang them." But journalists put theirs on the front page.

When a couple of delegates walked out of the conference in protest against its purpose, the news of their act was banned in India.

The government, already awash in slogans and catch phrases like "The ex-colonialists denigrate the Indian achievements for their own purpose," "C. I. A. conspiracy," "Standing on our own feet," "National integrity, national unity," and "Only the stick works in India," soon began in earnest to generate its own Orwellian Newspeak. David Selbourne, who visited India not long after the Emergency was proclaimed, noted in *Harper's* that professors at universities described their colleagues in prison as being "temporarily out of station," and that a university chancellor explained the forced peace on his campus in this way: "The tide of indiscipline has been turned; we have recovered our bright image." A ban on all strikes and picketing was presented as "the fight against Fascism." The establishment of forced-labor camps for lepers and beggars was described as "the struggle against the evil forces threatening India." Granting new tax concessions to the wealthy in the Emergency budget was described as "ending the tax privileges of the rich." And the Minister for Information and Broadcasting called the government's monopoly of news and comment "restructuring the entire newspaper industry so as to make it accountable to the people." Ubiquitous mammoth billboards quoted pithy sayings by Mrs. Gandhi, à la Chairman Mao—"The only cure for poverty is hard work," for instance, and "Discipline is the watchword of the hour" (implying that the hundreds of millions of poor and unemployed had only their indolence to blame for their plight). Government officials constantly proclaimed Mrs. Gandhi's "New India" to be freer and more democratic than the old, pre-Emergency India. On Independence Day in August, 1976, President Fakhruddin Ali Ahmed said, "We enter the thirtieth year of freedom. . . . It is only by a general acceptance of certain norms of conduct by all concerned that a new era of self-imposed discipline can dawn. . . . The proclamation of Emergency is neither to gain more power than what the constitution provides for nor to switch over from one system to another but to bring about such economic, social, and political changes as have become relevant and necessary in the interest of the people of India." Mrs. Gandhi also met with considerable success in exporting her brand of Newspeak; in the spring of

1976 John Jacob, the president of the Singapore Indian Congress Party, described the Emergency as "the magnificent changes that have come upon India today," and said that they "must be seen to be believed."

With the proclamation of the Emergency, the Ministry of Information and Broadcasting—or, rather, its Directorate of Advertising and Visual Publicity—began busily bringing out pamphlets that attacked the immoral excesses and the conspiratorial designs of the opposition parties. One pamphlet was aimed at the Muslim party Jamaat-e-Islami, saying, "Its religious fanaticism and separatist mentality strengthened the reactionary and Fascist forces in the country," while a companion pamphlet excoriated the Hindu party Jana Sangh for, among other things, advocating the forcible assimilation of Muslims into the dominant Hindu culture. A pamphlet on the Communist Party of India (Marxist-Leninist), the Naxalites, used violent language to describe the Party's advocacy of violent revolution: "Hacking persons to death, playing football with severed heads, and drenching oneself in the blood of an exploiter were all justified by the CPI (ML) leadership." The pamphlet went on to implicate Jaya Prakash Narayan, a pacifist, in such bloody politics, using the technique of guilt by association: "When Jaya Prakash Narayan launched his [1974 nonviolent] 'total revolution' programme, among the strange bedfellows in his company were the Naxalites, against whom only three years ago he had carried out a blistering campaign. JP [Jaya Prakash] had long discussions with the various factions of the CPI (ML) in Patna and Calcutta and enlisted their support. Bolstered by the safe cover provided by the JP-led movement, the Naxalites once again became active in parts of Bihar and unleashed their cult of terror and violence, resulting in the deaths of seven policemen."

But the Ministry discharged even more venom against the religious-political fringe movement called Anand Marg (Path of Bliss), formed around Prabhat Ranjan Sarkar, a sometime railway accountant turned would-be messiah and known to his worshipping devotees as Anandmurtiji. The movement, founded in 1955, grew so rapidly that by the mid-seventies its membership numbered in the millions, and it had centers all over the world. Strangely, many of its devotees in India were government servants, and this may be why the Ministry singled it out for special attention. The government's case against Anand Marg—and Anandmurtiji—was set forth in a pamphlet with the brazen title "Soiling the Saffron Robe," which was supposedly written by a former Anand Marg member, one Nawal Kishore, who was identified as an ex-instructor and ex-performer of "rites with human skulls." The pamphlet said, "With such a personality cult as its basis, one should not be surprised if Anand Marg preaches stark dictatorship. . . . This concept of benevolent [*sic*] dictatorship smacks of Nazi ideology to a disgusting degree. . . . Anandmurtiji has, the devotees are told, no . . . weaknesses, and his appearance on the scene pronounces the advent of a messiah." The pamphlet later quoted a statement of condemnation ostensibly made by Sarkar's estranged wife, Uma, in 1971: "He regards himself as a parallel to God. . . . But his greed knows no bounds. . . . He did not create spiritual aspirants from among those boys whom he lured for a spiritual life. He began to engage them in different filthy acts." Mrs. Sarkar went on to allege in her statement, which ran to several pages, that if her husband's devotees refused to do his bidding or were disloyal to him he tortured them or had them murdered. She said that her husband would charm innocent young boys, persuading them that they were girls in their previous incarnation, and then use them as his homosexual partners. She said that he was so filled with self-importance and grandiose notions that he fancied he was better than "all art and literature of the world, all the great souls and saints, all geniuses." He made no secret of the fact that his ambition was "to become the emperor of the world." For several years, she watched with silent incredulity his religious and sexual antics, finally concluding that he was actually an odious criminal, at which point she "bade him goodbye" and, taking their only child, a son, went into the world penniless but convinced that she was doing the right thing. "From that hour we are shelterless and completely insecure," she said. The pamphlet then gave this already incredible tale a strange twist, linking the movement with a C.I.A. spy and a United States government conspiracy. After noting that Sarkar and many of his disciples—called Margis—had been arrested and charged with murders, the pamphlet stated:

> In 1973, top Margis met in a conference in Katmandu and drew up plans to meet the situation arising out of the arrest of P. R. Sarkar. One of the key persons to attend this conclave was one Judie Marchel, a Harvard scholar, who joined the Marg while she was in Manila. At the instance of Avadhut Bimalanand, who had gone to the Philippines as Sarkar's emissary, she came to India in 1969 and stayed on. Soon she got very close to Anandmurti and took up the name Madhuri.
>
> The exact whereabouts of Judie Marchel are not presently known, but it may not be too farfetched to surmise that she had links with the notorious American agency. However, it is reliably learnt that she has been launching a tirade against the Indian Government from Hong Kong and big cities of the U.S.A.

A Canadian lawyer, Claude-Armand Sheppard, visited India in behalf of the International Commission of Jurists, in Geneva, and the International League for Human Rights, in New York, in order to observe some of the court proceedings against Sarkar and his followers. In a report forwarded to his sponsors, he maintained that although in the conduct of this particular case the government continued to follow the legal niceties in "the finest British tradition," the conditions of the Emergency made it almost impossible for the defendants to obtain justice. In the Kafka-esque atmosphere of a police state, Sheppard said, witnesses were afraid to come forward, others were in hiding, still others were in jail themselves. "In other words," he observed, "the accused not only have arrayed against them the entire power of the Indian police establishment, but even if they had all the funds necessary to prepare an adequate defense, it is highly unlikely that they could find, or if they found them could produce, witnesses willing to testify on their behalf."

In December of 1976, Sarkar and his devotees were found guilty.

Sarkar and company, of course, shared their predicament with the leaders of other opposition groups and parties. And, under the Emergency, the ordinary citizen ceased to be any better off, having been stripped of his legal protection and remedies. He ceased to enjoy any of his constitutional freedoms: freedom of speech and assembly, of forming associations or unions, of travelling and living in any part of India; freedom to acquire, hold, and dispose of property; freedom to practice the trade or occupation of his choice. Deprived by the government, with the concurrence of the Supreme Court, of what had theretofore been considered the most fundamental right of all—the right of habeas corpus—he was left defenseless.

In the meantime, the government continued to build up a statutory and constitutional foundation for formalizing its arrogation of power to itself, in the event that the Emergency should be lifted. It so altered the Maintenance of Internal Security Act and the Conservation of Foreign Exchange and Prevention of Smuggling Activities Act that it could thenceforward detain any person for two years—generally for any crime and specifically for economic crimes—without supplying him or a court with grounds for his detention. Moreover, to rein in the middle class it enacted, among other laws, the Urban Land Ceiling Regulation Act, restricting the amount of land an individual could own in a city.

At the district level, the local political institutions were undermined and their powers assumed by government offices. At the state level, two governments controlled by opposition parties—those of Tamil Nadu (formerly Madras) and Gujarat—were dismissed, and this meant that all the states had been placed either directly or indirectly under Congress Party control. In the government, the power was concentrated in an increasingly centralized bureaucracy, whose top echelons depended for their influence less on seniority, as before, than on Mrs. Gandhi's favor. In fact, Mrs. Gandhi transformed the constitutional apparatus around the Prime Minister into the monolithic machinery of a personal dictatorship: the Prime Minister's Secretariat became the engine of the government, and the Research and Analysis Wing of the Secretariat became her far-flung intelligence network. The Border Security Force, a paramilitary corps numbering some two hundred and fifty thousand, was newly quartered in major Indian cities and also functioned almost as a praetorian guard. The police force was purged, and some thousands of its officers were "retired in the public interest." Most significant of all, the nine hundred thousand men in the armed forces—the world's fourth-largest—were placed under the tight personal control of the Prime Minister.

The Emergency amendments were written into the constitution wholesale, without recourse to a Constituent Assembly. The government was able to rewrite the constitution in this way because some of the opposition members of Parliament—and even some dissident Congress Party members—were in jail, and because Mrs. Gandhi's Supreme Court failed to insist that Parliament's power to amend the constitution was not absolute. (The Supreme Court had earlier held that the constitution's basic structure could not be altered by constitutional amendment, but it never defined that basic structure.) Early in 1976, the Congress Party went as far as to establish a committee to suggest still other amendments. One suggestion by this group, known as the Swaran Singh Committee (it was named after the former Minister of Defense), was that the constitution be so amended that the courts would no longer have the power to review the substance of any constitutional amendment. Mrs. Gandhi not only adopted the proposal but went a step further: that September, her government introduced in Parliament a bill—the Forty-fourth Amendment bill, which was one of half a dozen such amendment bills following the proclamation of the Emergency—that would do away once and for all with the old system of constitutional checks and balances among the Parliament, the judiciary, and the executive in favor of outright executive autocracy. (Later, this amendment and the two amendments preceding it were consolidated as the Forty-second Amendment.) The courts as a whole would no longer have the authority to review the constitutionality of any law; the Supreme Court would be an exception, but even there a two-thirds majority would be required to strike down any law. No court whatever would have the authority to review the constitutionality of any amendment, and the President, merely on the personal advice of the Prime Minister—without consultation with the Cabinet, for instance—would be able to place any particular state or region under emergency rule at any time. In November, the lower house of Parliament passed the amendment bill. Subsequently, the largely ceremonial upper house gave its approval, and the state legislatures ratified the amendment.

Mrs. Gandhi's emerging dictatorship was reminiscent of Mussolini's and Stalin's, and possibly even Hitler's in the early years. Though Mrs. Gandhi's personality bore no resemblance whatever to Hitler's, in many ways her actions both leading up to the Emergency and under it recalled Hitler's in 1933. Hitler blamed a conspiracy of the opposition for his emergency; so did Mrs. Gandhi for hers. Hitler became Chancellor of Germany with the reluctant assent of President Paul von Hindenburg; Mrs. Gandhi might have experienced considerable difficulty in having the Emergency proclaimed if President Fakhruddin Ali Ahmed had been a strong man and had resisted her directive. Hitler claimed that he was suspending the political process to realize social and economic ends; Mrs. Gandhi made the same claim. Hitler's civil servants and military officers continued to obey him, sometimes against their better judgment; so did Mrs. Gandhi's. In fact, Mrs. Gandhi's emergency measures faintly echoed those of Hitler. (Hitler's decree suspending the individual guarantees under the Weimar constitution read, in part, "Thus, restrictions on personal liberty, on the right of free expression of opinion, including freedom of the press; on the rights of assembly and association;

violations of the privacy of postal, telegraphic, and telephonic communications; warrants for house searches; orders for confiscation, as well as restrictions on property, are permissible beyond the legal limits otherwise prescribed.") Hitler used his emergency to rout the opposition and to reorganize the government and the economy; this was how Mrs. Gandhi used hers. Mrs. Gandhi's constitution for the "New India" resembled Hitler's so-called Enabling Law. She often made allegations that the opposition, financed and goaded by foreign powers, was destroying India, and such statements recalled Hitler's seductive claim that Germany had been defeated in the First World War by a "stab in the back." Indeed, Mrs. Gandhi might have been ushering in an Indian version of Hitler's National Socialist regime, with private ownership of industry, farms, and service enterprises under state guidance. Even before the Emergency, the Indian state was the most powerful organization in the country, employing perhaps as much as a third of the work force, and serving as a patron of social, economic, and cultural bodies. It always had a cozy relationship not only with industry and commerce but also with all institutions of art and learning. Under the Emergency, the corporate state, personified by Mrs. Gandhi, came into its own.

# 4

# Apologists
and Critics

In a magazine article written in 1975, Mrs. Gandhi claimed that through the Emergency she had streamlined Indian democracy to reflect the Indian reality better and to make it more responsive to the needs of the poor. "Preserving the integrity of the fabric is a major challenge in the early years of any new nation," she wrote. "Our constitution-makers were fully aware of the problems involved and knew that although our diversity had to be accommodated through federalist provisions, the center should hold at all times and should have sufficient power to deal with threats to unity and order." Though the opposition parties constituted a small minority in the Parliament, she claimed that they were so irresponsible that she had reason to fear for Indian democracy. She said that if she had not proclaimed the Emergency, the opposition would have destroyed democracy by extra-constitutional means. "Democracy meant responsibility, not license for everyone," she wrote. "The government's responsibility was to allow freedom of speech and association, but the opposition and citizens had also the responsibility of not paralyzing government functioning. But what was happening here was not just freedom but license. And I think democracy was being destroyed by taking advantage of the freedom which democracy gives, especially as some of these parties who are against us have never claimed to believe in democracy."

On another occasion, she elaborated on this theme:

Democracy has two obligations. There are obligations on the government that it should allow free press, free speech, and association, and so on, but it also [places] an obligation on the others to observe the rules of the game, if you like, but that was not being done. . . . It was not a question of the entire country wanting something. It was a small minority. Elections were only a few months to go and had they waited they would have had the verdict of the people. But one of the opposition leaders said, "This will have to be fought out on the streets." Another one said, "There has to be total revolution," and he tried to incite not only the industrial workers but the Army and the police. Now this could not have strengthened democracy in any way. If the people feel that their needs are not being met and their lives are being constantly disturbed, and I mean the mass of the people, then that poses very grave danger to the system.

She claimed that through the Emergency she had also modernized the Indian judicial system, which, because it was inherited from the British, served essentially middle-class interests, equating liberty with property, and placing more emphasis on protecting the rights of individuals than on furthering social justice. Indeed, she blamed the judicial system for frustrating many of the government's efforts to carry out social and economic reforms, such as distribution of land, abolition of feudal privileges, and dissolution of the monopolies of a few business families. She looked to the Emergency to usher in a speedier and more revolutionary system of justice, claiming that the individual liberties and rights she had abridged had meaning only for the middle class, and that the equality of opportunity she was now trying to insure had meaning for the poor. "What is not understood by some of our casual critics is that the political and social institutions of a nation should meet the immediate and large-term requirements of that nation," she said. She also asserted that her radical measures had precedents in other former Western colonies. Like India, many of those colonies, when they were granted independence, established Western-type parliamentary democracies, but, as one of her most trusted spokesmen, B. K. Nehru (a distant cousin), explained in a university lecture, they all found it necessary long before India did to curtail their democracies in favor of indigenous systems, usually with "a much stronger and stabler executive" than the Western model allowed, sometimes even "at the cost of democracy itself." In her view, as it was expressed by B. K. Nehru, the main reason for such changes was that "the basic problem of the people of the poor and underdeveloped countries is very different from that of Western Europe and the white dominions of the Commonwealth, where parliamentary democracy has been a success." He went on, "This is the problem of the removal of poverty, which in some countries, such as India, has achieved proportions which are unimaginable in the Western world. For the vast majority of people in such countries the democratic freedoms, which so delight the hearts of the Western-influenced urban intellectual, have no meaning whatsoever." Mrs. Gandhi praised the Emergency for putting an end to wasteful social and economic disruptions and for fostering a new sense of national discipline and a climate for economic progress. "No country can advance without discipline," she observed. "So either the people must do it themselves or the government has to do it. . . . This emergency has created a spirit of discipline without any exhortation on our side. And we hope to use this new spirit to increase production and to undertake many new programs which had become difficult before because of the cynicism which was being spread by some of our newspapers."

Supporters of Mrs. Gandhi's coup liked to point to the changes made in other Third World countries over the years. Sooner or later, these people said, all the countries had to resort to emergency rule, to "guided democracy," to one-party rule, to civil or military dictatorship, or to Communism, and they noted that even the Philippines, once a stable Asian democracy, had succumbed to dictatorship. They said that the failure of Western-type liberal democracy in one poor country after another was inevitable: that democracy was a foreign transplant kept alive by a native élite who had inherited not only liberal values but power from their colonial masters; that the authoritarianism of the Communist East was better suited to a poor country than the free institutions of the democratic West; that the Soviet Union, which in the course of just over half a century rose from being one of the most backward countries in the world to become one of its two superpowers, had more to teach a poor country than any of the advanced Western countries had; that the Western countries continued to be associated in the minds of the poor with imperialism, in part because of the British policies in what became Malaysia, the French policies in Algeria and Indo-China, and the American policies in Vietnam, while the Soviet Union's domination of Eastern Europe had never been understood as imperialistic. The more sophisticated defenders of the Emergency came up with an economic rationale: since without the investment of capital, which represents the difference between current production and current consumption, there can be no increase in either production or material wealth, and since current production in a poor country is so abysmally low that all of it vanishes in current consumption, a government must take Draconian measures to keep current consumption stable, or actually reduce it, in order to generate savings and capital for investment—something impossible in a democracy, where the government can be voted out of office.

B. K. Nehru wrote:

> Political parties in a democracy must necessarily vie with each other to increase public expenditure, raise wages and salaries, and decrease taxation. . . . Contrast what happens under a system in which the executive government is not removable by the popular will—in a dictatorship. . . . The gap between production and consumption is initially increased by reducing consumption without regard to the intensity of the suffering [of the poor]. In the early days of the Soviet Union, [this] reduction in consumption was sometimes so great as to

have caused death by famine. . . . This increased production is not allowed to be consumed but is again compulsorily saved and reinvested. The compounded result of this process, repeated year after year, is rapidly to increase the gross national product of the country, though its people continue to remain as poor and deprived as before. A rise in their standard of living is not permitted till such time as the rulers think that a sufficient rate of saving—and of growth—can be maintained, even if consumption is allowed to rise.

Supporters of Mrs. Gandhi's Emergency, like B. K. Nehru, argued that such a capital shortage can be alleviated in a poor country neither by the attraction of private foreign investment, which smacks of economic imperialism, and which, in any case, is not likely, because investors have more secure havens close to home, nor by an increase in trade, which seems impossible as long as the poor country is forced, as most poor countries are, to trade its comparatively cheap raw materials for expensive Western machinery and manufactured goods (scarcely any raw materials except oil are so basic as to permit the establishment of an effective cartel), nor by reliance on more foreign aid, which is likely to dry up as the Western countries become increasingly preoccupied with their own economic problems. A poor country, therefore, has no choice but to stand on its own feet, neglected and unaided, and try to bring about an economic revolution by totalitarian means, repugnant though they may be to the democratic conscience. These supporters contended, moreover, that in a poor country where few can read or write reform must, by its very nature, be paternalistic, and requires some sort of totalitarian shortcut. In their eyes, a political system could be only a means to an end—the eradication of poverty. They would write off the courts and Parliament, a free press, and other accoutrements of an open society as obstacles to reform—mere bourgeois luxuries. And, in any event, they maintained, the conditions in democratic India had so deteriorated that the country was all but ungovernable.

It is true that at the time of the Emergency forty per cent of the population had fallen below the government's poverty line of the absolute minimal conditions for mere survival. The five five-year plans for economic development which had been initiated since 1951 had only helped to make the rich richer and the poor poorer. The emphasis in the early plans had been on heavy industry, such as steel plants, in the belief that that was the quickest way to industrialize the country and raise the standard of living. In the later plans, the emphasis had been shifted to agriculture—for instance, to irrigation projects—but the shift had come so gradually and so halfheartedly that it had not had a chance to have much effect on the poor. The much heralded green revolution had ended up benefitting mostly the rich landlords, who had big tracts of land and could afford expensive fertilizers. And a series of droughts in the early nineteen-seventies, a world-wide recession, and, of course, the jump in oil prices had all worked to produce acute shortages and spiralling inflation. Partly as a result, the migration from the villages to the cities had continued, adding to the ranks of the unregenerate urban poor—the pavement dwellers, the beggars, the malcontents. In the cities, party organizers and labor leaders were not above using the politics of agitation to build up personal followings. They would call out their supporters on strikes and picket lines at the slightest excuse, shutting down shops, offices, universities, steel plants, power plants, railways, airlines. Sometimes the shutdowns were intended to protest a government or business action, but more often they were intended merely to show political muscle. The businessmen or government officials who were the targets of such shutdowns were mostly able to insulate themselves against the economic consequences, so the real victims were the day laborers, like hawkers and coolies, who had no resources to tide them over. Political agitation had become so routine that it had almost evolved into a form of self-expression, a national culture in itself. But in reality this culture was only a reflection of the people's impotence. In the meantime, across the country industrial production was declining and public services were falling apart.

Mrs. Gandhi's coup met practically no resistance, in part

because democracy had been used to mask what was actually an oligarchy. This oligarchy represented the middle class, and this middle class, mostly urban, included only somewhere between three and fifteen per cent of the total population, depending on the economic criteria one uses. In any event, the powerless poor, who had never had a stake in the government, were steadily increasing, and overwhelming the middle class. At the same time, the five general elections since independence had shown that the government was becoming more and more a hostage of ever-narrowing caste and class interests—of self-serving politicians, administrators, businessmen, landlords, and Brahmans. The Congress Party was smug, complacent, and decadent, whereas the opposition parties, despite a show of unity just before the Emergency, were weak and fragmented, in part because their experience of power was limited to the ruling of an occasional state. Their members were constantly changing their political affiliation or founding splinter parties, sometimes around demagogic leaders with extremist ideologies. Even Parliament and the state legislatures had become notorious for disorder; their members would brawl on the floor of the house, and on occasion actually hurl brickbats or use physical intimidation to prevent Ministers and party leaders from discharging their duties. Whenever Parliament and the legislatures mobilized themselves and enacted a piece of daring social legislation, such as land reform, it would be circumvented: either the land-reform legislation would be tied up in the courts for years by landlords or, if it put a ceiling on the size of holdings, the land would simply be subdivided among the landlords' families. Not only Parliament and the legislatures but also the courts were dominated by middle-class interests, and used procedures and language that bore little relation to the needs of the poor. The law was being brought into increasing disrepute, the business of governing made more difficult. As anarchy and lawlessness spread, in and out of the government, power became increasingly concentrated in Delhi. When a state proved incapable of governing itself, the central government, using the emergency provisions of the constitution, took the state's government over. One result of such moves was that the leaders of states still governing themselves were so fearful of losing their authority and power to the central government that they often functioned as a kind of cat's-paw for the Prime Minister.

Following the proclamation of the Emergency, Mrs. Gandhi's supporters began daily parading its gains. They said that the Emergency had given the country a new sense of purpose; that its extraordinary powers had brought to heel corrupt officials, black marketeers, tax evaders, smugglers, and unscrupulous union leaders; that it had ended strikes, picketing, and absenteeism. Furthermore, they said, the power of landlords and moneylenders had been cut down, and bonded peasants given relief from their debts. The Emergency had made it possible to distribute some land to the landless in the villages. It had made it possible to undertake urban land development: beggars, pavement squatters, and slum dwellers were rounded up and given gainful employment in public projects. Even the rate of inflation had been brought down precipitously within a year—from about thirty per cent to ten. These supporters went on to make claims that were even more extravagant. They said that for the first time both private and public industries were functioning well; that the universities had been revived as centers of learning; that judicial hairsplitting and litigious delays had been done away with. The Emergency, according to them, had relieved business and government from political agitation and partisan pressures, and thereby lifted morale, allowing the government to pursue pragmatic economic policies, whether these were associated with the left or with the right. For example, while pursuing such socialist policies as land reform the government was also able to liberalize licensing regulations for businessmen and offer budgetary incentives to foreign investors. The consequent increase in the flow of exports was partly responsible for an increase in foreign exchange, which the country had needed in order to import oil and technology. International agencies and Western governments had come to contribute about two billion dollars a year, or one-sixth of India's national budget, in loans and grants. Following the proclamation of the Emergency, its supporters said, economic and political conditions were judged to be so stable that the World Bank was advocating more foreign investment in India.

The Emergency's critics, many of them Indians who had previously settled abroad or who fled after the Emergency was proclaimed, rejected all the arguments of its supporters. They said that Mrs. Gandhi was exploiting the issue of poverty for her own selfish ends and as diversionary tactics for avoiding real reform—in short, as window dressing for dictatorship. If Western-type democracy was unsuited to India, the critics asked, why did the Prime Minister still keep up the pretense of democracy? They said that her lip service to constitutional niceties was intended to give her coup an aura of respectability and legitimacy, in an attempt to insure the loyalty of the armed forces. Some of her critics believed that the prolongation of the Emergency into a second year put her legitimacy in doubt, and wondered whether the Indian armed forces would continue to be loyal to her much longer.

However, those armed forces, schooled in the British apolitical tradition, never ceased to adhere to the principle of civilian control. Indeed, the high-ranking officers remained careful to model themselves on their British mentors, functioning as a race apart, and being known for their polo playing, their hard drinking, and their stiffly pressed uniforms. The rank and file, for their part, though they were often from poor backgrounds, were known for their discipline, their patriotism, and their heroism, which they had demonstrated in the several wars since independence. The fact is that the Emergency had been very popular with both the officers and many of the rank and file, who, like other members of the middle class, had seen a threat to their privileges in the opposition parties' stirring up of mass discontent, and who, in any case, were divided from one another by race, region, religion, and caste, and so were probably incapable of any concerted political action. Yet if Mrs. Gandhi had actually tried to put through the social and economic reforms she kept talking about, she might have ended up arousing among them the same degree of antagonism that was being displayed by the opposition parties. Practically every other Asian or African country that started out as a free society with apolitical armed forces sooner or later succumbed to military dictatorship. It might be that in India, as elsewhere, to overthrow the established government the armed forces would need no greater provocation than the wish to put one of their own men in power—and, perhaps for this reason, one of Mrs. Gandhi's first actions after the Emergency was proclaimed was to put old Field Marshal Sam Manekshaw, a sixty-one-year-old hero of the Bangladesh war, who had retired as chief of staff of the Army, under temporary house arrest.

In any event, for some time before the Emergency was proclaimed there were signs of restiveness both in the military and in government circles generally. For one thing, Mrs. Gandhi, disregarding the tradition of the seniority system, had reached over the heads of several generals to appoint General Tapeshwar Nath Raina the Army chief of staff—much as she had reached over the heads of three senior judges to appoint Ray the Chief Justice of India. (Both men were deemed personally loyal to her.) For another thing, the power of the Border Security Force and of the Central Intelligence Bureau within the government had been growing at an ominous rate. The Border Security Force had been established in 1962, after the India-China war, to patrol and guard the India-China border, but lately it had been used as a paramilitary force to maintain internal security. Similarly, the Central Intelligence Bureau had been used increasingly throughout the country as a political arm of the government, and surveillance—through telephone taps, mail checks, and house watches— of government officials and of politicians had become routine. The Emergency, in effect, licensed such government efforts to stamp out all dissent. Even in Mrs. Gandhi's own Congress Party, suppression of dissent was carried to such lengths under the Emergency that the Party president, Barooah, noted that it had brought about a "qualitative change" in politics, so that thenceforth

Party members were "not to ask questions but to carry out orders."

The critics conceded some of the Emergency's gains, but claimed that these were short-lived and actually pointed to signs of a return of pre-Emergency troubles. After nineteen months, they said, inflation was heating up again; there had been rises in the prices of coal, steel, cement, textiles, and food grains. (In any case, some said, the inflation had been brought under control a year before the Emergency was proclaimed—in the spring of 1974, when the government broke the national strike of the railway workers' union.) These critics maintained that the political arguments of Mrs. Gandhi's supporters might explain the reasons for a poor country's turning to Communism but not the reasons for its turning to military or personal dictatorship, and they dismissed the economic argument as beside the point and obfuscatory: not only did the argument ignore the fact that capital shortage was a universal condition but it blithely assumed that a given poor country had at some point been hospitable to democracy, when in fact most poor countries had never known anything better than oligarchy—a system whose leaders had never hesitated to take totalitarian measures in their own interests. The critics declared that the Emergency could not offer even a temporary solution to India's basic problem—providing the unemployed and the landless peasants with work, which in an agrarian society must be in agriculture. Mrs. Gandhi, they said, could not expect much further help on a large scale from the governments of Western democracies, whose people were philosophically opposed to the Emergency; from the Soviet Union, which had not been known for its generosity in the matter of economic aid; or from the multinational corporations, which could make more money from their investments in South America and in other parts of Asia than they could from any investment in the much more inefficient and impoverished India, and which, in any case, tended to invest in mechanization—something that in India would have the effect of increas-

ing unemployment and poverty. The critics said that over a prolonged period the Emergency had closed off safety valves for
discontent and had so encouraged forces of Balkanization in the
country that it deprived the opposition parties of necessary
means of again taking an active part in regular politics, and that,
indeed, it provided the Congress Party with an opportunity to
decimate them, and so made many in the ranks of the opposition parties turn in desperation to thoughts of violent revolution; that although the leadership of the pro-Soviet Communist
Party of India had supported Mrs. Gandhi officially in the early
months of the Emergency, apparently under orders from the
Soviet Union, some of the rank and file of the Party later began
quietly drifting away to join the pro-Chinese Communist Party
of India (Marxist-Leninist), which had never had any use for
Mrs. Gandhi. The critics contended, further, that the Emergency had transferred power from an oligarchy to a cabal, from
caste and class to family and family dynasty, and thereby further
centralized the government and divorced it from the governed.
They said that the rise of Sanjay as heir apparent and the rewrit-
ing of the constitution had institutionalized the Emergency into
a form of tyranny, and that the suspension of habeas corpus, in
particular, had left everyone open to harassment and persecu-
tion by petty officials, even in matters unrelated to politics—
that, in fact, without habeas corpus every constable was poten-
tially a petty dictator, in his way as powerful as the Prime Minister or her son. The Emergency had so streamlined the channels
of bribery and corruption that there were now fewer people to
buy off, and, without the fear of Parliamentary, public, or legal
consequences, those few could deliver more. Indeed, instead of
removing the existing inequities the Emergency might have introduced new ones. Moreover, the Muslims, who had formerly
regarded Mrs. Gandhi as their defender and had seen in the
Emergency a check to Hindu dominance, had subsequently become alarmed by the government's nearly year-old campaign
for sterilization to control population, which they regarded as an
anti-Muslim offensive. Many of the poor in the cities, who had

also seen in Nehru's daughter a personal champion, had subsequently become embittered and discontented because they had been separated from their homes and livelihoods—such as they were—and made to live in what were essentially forced-labor camps.

Some critics even argued that Mrs. Gandhi's record as a whole—her Prime Ministership had lasted more than a decade—was dismal. Ashok Mitra, a respected Indian economist, speaking freely from England, where he spent a year at the University of Sussex, noted in an interview he gave to the Washington *Post* that during her regime per-capita income had failed to rise, industrial production had risen less than three per cent per year, and farm production had risen by only one per cent per year. (In the preceding ten years, industrial production and farm production had annually risen at least eight per cent and three and four-tenths per cent, respectively.) Mitra said that Mrs. Gandhi's record since the Emergency began had been no better. It was true that she had redistributed some land to landless farmers, but the amount distributed was only seven hundred thousand acres, or less than two-tenths of one per cent of India's total of four hundred million acres under cultivation. Instead of freeing the debt-ridden peasants by cancelling their debts outright, as her left-wing supporters were urging her to do, she had only imposed a debt moratorium. The real beneficiaries of her Emergency rule had been the landlords and moneylenders. Mitra maintained that many of the other ostensible gains of the Emergency—like the Twenty-Point Program for economic development, which was essentially socialist, and which Mrs. Gandhi announced during the first days of the Emergency—were more rhetorical than substantive, and, in any case, did not require her to resort to emergency measures. The economic gains that there had been—most notably, huge surpluses in food grains—were due more to a succession of extraordinarily good monsoons than to the Emergency, but Mitra felt that the government would believe its own propaganda and take credit for the surpluses. Mrinal Datta-Chaudhuri, writing in the final issue of the

Indian monthly *Seminar,* which was compelled by the government to suspend publication in July of 1976, made the same point: "It is not true that propaganda works on its intended victims alone; it can also create powerful self-delusions."

Mrs. Gandhi said repeatedly that she had no choice but to proclaim the Emergency, because there was a "conspiracy" of "the opposition" to bring her and her constitutionally elected government down by unconstitutional, extra-Parliamentary political agitation—by a mass national uprising springing from the so-called people's movement. She claimed that what "the opposition" had failed to achieve constitutionally at the polls since independence it was trying just before the Emergency to achieve through political agitation. In support of this claim, she pointed to the fortnight of opposition-led "Resign, Indira" rallies in Delhi between the time of her conviction and the Emergency, and, specifically, to the much discussed public rally on the eve of the Emergency. It was at this rally that she was put on notice that if she did not voluntarily resign there would be week-long nonviolent resistance—protest marches, picketing, strikes—and at this rally that Jaya Prakash Narayan issued his supposed call for mutiny. But there was a question whether those rallies, exhortations, and threats amounted to a conspiracy, and even whether there was such a thing as "the opposition." In letters and articles subsequently smuggled out of the country, the leaders of the opposition parties insisted that "the opposition" was Mrs. Gandhi's bugaboo—that, at most, it was a loose temporary alliance of some minority parties. They said that their "Resign, Indira" rallies and the planned protest movement were in the hallowed tradition of Mahatma Gandhi and the independence struggle, and that, in any case, for a "felon" to continue as Prime Minister was an affront to the democratic system. Moreover, they said, it was a universally accepted principle, confirmed by the Nazi war criminals' trial at Nuremberg, and even, possibly, by Lieutenant William Calley's trial at Fort Benning, that it was not incumbent on any man to carry out illegal orders; before the Emergency, Jaya Prakash Narayan had witnessed policemen in his own state of Bihar mowing down innocent bystanders and students, and he did not want a repetition of it in Delhi. The leaders of the opposition parties were quoted in underground pamphlets as saying that the protest campaign was directed against Mrs. Gandhi, not against the government or against democracy. In the view of these leaders, she was herself at the head of a conspiracy, which was intended to frame them and to establish a constitutional dictatorship—the most difficult form of government to dislodge. Not surprisingly, Mrs. Gandhi never missed an opportunity over the ensuing months to proclaim that all her Emergency measures were constitutional and that India was still a democracy. Like Humpty Dumpty in "Through the Looking-Glass," she seemed to be saying that when she used a word it meant just what she chose it to mean—neither more nor less. M. C. Chagla, a retired public servant who had been a Chief Justice of the Bombay High Court and also Minister of External Affairs in Mrs. Gandhi's government, and who under the Emergency suddenly found himself in the "opposition" camp, observed after the transformation, "The curious thing is this—we are accused of being Fascists, of being 'right revisionists.' . . . They are the democrats. I do not think that there can be a greater linguistic perversity than to call us Fascists and call themselves democrats." (Chagla delivered these remarks—which were eventually published abroad—at a conference in Ahmadabad, in Gujarat, before Mrs. Gandhi dissolved the state's opposition government. He was not unmindful of the risks he was running: "Anybody like you and me may be shut behind the bars . . . and they need not tell me why they shut me up, and might give the reason that I have delivered this speech today.")

Jaya Prakash Narayan, one of the first "opposition" members to be taken prisoner under the Emergency, was in his seventies, and so sick—he had been a diabetic for many years—that after four and a half months he was released. Thenceforward, his political activities were much curtailed, not only because of the Emergency but also because of a kidney condition that forced him to spend almost every second day attached to a dialysis machine. But he remained a passionate critic of Mrs. Gandhi. He wrote a letter to her on December 5, 1975, which immediately started circulating in the underground, and which surfaced two months later in *The Far Eastern Economic Review,* published in Hong Kong. In the letter, he said that the so-called people's movement, far from being a general uprising, was restricted to one state, Bihar, and that his and the movement's aims, far from being revolutionary, were to improve the food-distribution system, check corruption, carry out land-reform legislation, work to improve the condition of the Untouchables, and curb social evils connected with divorce and the dowry—aims not unlike the professed aims of the Emergency. "Thus, the plan of which you speak . . . is a figment of your imagination thought up to justify your totalitarian measures," he wrote to Mrs. Gandhi. He scolded her like a father, telling her that she must have a "guilty conscience" or she would not feel the need to air daily her spurious reasons for proclaiming the Emergency. He was certain, however, that she would not succeed in her efforts to "damn the opposition to political perdition," because, he said, he had faith in the good sense of the people. He continued:

> You are reported to have said that democracy is not more important than the nation. Are you not presuming too much, Madam Prime Minister? You are not the only one who cares for the nation. Among those whom you have detained or imprisoned there are many who have done as much for the nation as you. And every one of them is as good a patriot as yourself. So please do not apply salt to our wounds by lecturing to us about the nation.
>
> Moreover, it is a false choice that you have formulated. There is no choice between democracy and the nation.

After remarking that a democratic constitution could be changed only by a Constituent Assembly, not by emergency decrees, laws, and constitutional amendments, Narayan wrote:

> If Justice, Liberty, Equality, and Fraternity have not been rendered to "all its citizens" [as was mandated by the constitution] even after a quarter of a century of signing of that Constitution, the fault is not that of the Constitution or of democracy but of the Congress Party that has been in power in Delhi all these years. It is precisely because of that failure that there is so much unrest among the people and the youth. Repression is no remedy for that. . . . It only compounds the failure. . . .
>
> Having performed this unpleasant duty, may I conclude with a few parting words of advice? You know I am an old man. My life's work is done. . . . I have given all my life . . . to the country and asked for nothing in return. So I shall be content to die a prisoner [he was speaking metaphorically] under your regime.
>
> Would you listen to the advice of such a man? Please do not destroy the foundations that the Fathers of the Nation, including your noble father, had laid down. There is nothing but strife and suffering along the path that you have taken. You inherited a great tradition, noble values, and a working democracy. Do not leave behind a miserable wreck of all that. It would take a long time to put all that together again. For it would be put together again, I have no doubt. A people who fought British imperialism and humbled it cannot accept indefinitely the indignity and shame of totalitarianism. The spirit of man can never be vanquished, no matter how deeply suppressed. In establishing your personal dictatorship you have buried it deep. But it will rise from the grave. Even in Russia it is slowly coming up.
>
> You have talked of social democracy. What a beautiful image those words call to the mind. But you have seen in eastern and central Europe how ugly is the reality: Naked dictatorship and in the ultimate analysis Russian overlordship. Please, please do not push India toward that terrible fate. . . .

You have accused the opposition and me of every kind of villainy. But let me assure you that if you do the right things—for instance . . . take the opposition into confidence, heed its advice—you will receive the willing cooperation of every one of us. For that you need not destroy democracy. The ball is in your court. It is for you to decide.

With these parting words, let me bid you farewell. May God be with you.

# 5

# Nehru Dynasty

Throughout Indian history, a few thousand people had, in effect, easily managed to rule millions of downtrodden, who always lived in fear of authority, cowed by a religion of fatalism. Even during the period of democracy, the government had had the air of a monarchy, with local satrapies dispensing patronage and favors. Indeed, the Congress Party, with its caste and class interests, had ruled the democracy at the center continuously. As Congress Party rule became virtually institutionalized, the rise and fall of many politicians had become increasingly dependent on the whim of the Prime Minister. In fact, the tone of the democracy had been set by the Nehru family, father and daughter, who, as Prime Ministers, ruled for all but nineteen months of the thirty years following independence, and that tone had been essentially princely.

"In my opinion, only two amendments to our constitution would suffice to make the whole of it completely progressive," S. K. Madhavan, one of Mrs. Gandhi's critics, caustically commented at an illegal meeting of citizens in Calcutta in June of 1976. "The first one should be 'I, Indira Gandhi, should continue to be the Prime Minister of India till my death'; the second one should be 'After me, my son Sanjay Gandhi should continue in that position till the end of his life.'" In 1928, when the future

Prime Minister Indira Gandhi was eleven years old, she eagerly watched as her regal grandfather Motilal Nehru was drawn in a carriage along a Calcutta street by thirty-four white horses ridden by thirty-four uniformed Congress Party volunteers. He was on his way to a session of the Congress Party. He was one of the most important leaders of the independence struggle and was the president of the Congress that year. A year afterward, she watched as her father, Jawaharlal Nehru, rode past on a white charger—very much the knight *sans peur et sans reproche.* He was surrounded by a detachment of Congress Party volunteers on horses and followed by a herd of elephants. He, too, was going to a Congress session, this time in Lahore. Later that day, she looked on proudly as her grandfather, much like a monarch passing on his crown and sceptre to his heir, stepped down from the Congress presidency in favor of his son. (It was the first time in the forty-five-year history of the Congress Party that a son had succeeded his father.) Within a few months, her grandfather was dead and her father was in prison.

From childhood, Indira felt herself destined for political life. She was a romantic girl living in a historic time of dramatic political struggle. As far back as she could remember, she had dreamed of becoming a second Joan of Arc. "Do you remember how fascinated you were when you first read the story of Jeanne d'Arc, and how your ambition was to be something like her?" her father wrote to her from prison in 1930. "If we are to be India's soldiers we have India's honor in our keeping, and that honor is a sacred trust. . . . One little test I shall ask you to apply whenever you are in doubt. . . . Never do anything in secret or anything that you would wish to hide. For the desire to hide anything means that you are afraid, and fear is a bad thing and unworthy of you. Be brave, and all the rest follows. . . . And if you do so, my dear, you will grow up a child of the light, unafraid and serene and unruffled, whatever may happen. . . . Goodbye, little one, and may you grow up into a brave soldier in India's service." (This was the first of a series of letters he wrote to her from prison over a period of three years; they were eventually published in a volume entitled "Glimpses of World History.")

Mrs. Gandhi, born in 1917, had a lonely and unsettled childhood. Her parents' marriage was seemingly not very happy. Her father was educated at Harrow and at Cambridge; her mother, Kamala, was unsophisticated and sketchily educated. Her father was in and out of British jails; her mother was sick much of the time with tuberculosis, and died when Indira was eighteen. Indira's formal education was inevitably neglected. Soon after her mother's death, she attended Oxford for a few months; she learned to play badminton there but did not put in much time on studies or sit for any examinations. While she was in England, however, she met a childhood friend, Feroze Gandhi (not related to Mahatma Gandhi), who was studying at the London School of Economics. They were married in 1942 in India, over the objections of the orthodox and the unorthodox alike, the latter including her father; she was a high-caste Kashmiri Brahman, and Feroze was not even a Hindu—he was a Parsi. They settled in Uttar Pradesh, where their sons were born—Rajiv in 1944, and Sanjay in 1946. The marriage proved to be a stormy one. After seven years, Indira left Feroze and went to live with her father in the Prime Minister's residence in Delhi, where she served as official hostess. There was an attempt at reconciliation some years later, during which Feroze also lived in the Prime Minister's residence, but it was unsuccessful.

Feroze, who resented being known as "the nation's son-in-law," made a name for himself as a journalist and a member of Parliament, and became a hero to critics of the Nehru government for his part in exposing the so-called Mundhra Affair, which was a *cause célèbre* in 1958. It concerned a stock transaction involving the industrialist Haridas Mundhra and the then Minister of Finance, T. T. Krishnamachari, who was eventually forced to resign. The newspaper-reading public avidly followed the hearings on the case, and for the first time in years the press and the opposition parties had an opportunity to thunder against corruption in Nehru's government. Nehru could have taken ruthless repressive measures against the critics, but instead he chose to allow them to have their say and the judicial inquiry to take its course, thus reminding the Ministers, as his biographer Michael Brecher observes, that in a democracy they were responsible to Parliament and the public at large. Feroze Gandhi died of a heart attack in 1960, at the age of forty-seven.

For most of the time that Nehru was Prime Minister, Indira lived with her widowed father, serving not only as his official hostess but as his confidante; she was his sole heir. In 1959, mainly because of her family's position in recent Indian history, she was given a major commission: she was made the president of the Congress Party. Her second major commission was when she was made Prime Minister, in 1966.

Although Nehru, despite his aristocratic background and natural inclinations, sought to conduct himself like a democrat, Mrs. Gandhi conducted herself increasingly like a queen. Certainly the politicians around her appeared to be courtiers. Her conduct may have stemmed from Nehru's position in modern India, from megalomania, or from a lack of self-awareness. In any event, following the proclamation of the Emergency she set about building herself a personality cult: billboards and buses everywhere were covered with signs and posters displaying her picture and quoting her sayings; the student branch of the Congress Party set to work organizing Indira Study Circles at universities; Congress politicians began widely circulating a new collection of her speeches and articles, entitled "India." (One of the commonest slogans heard in that period was "India is Indira, and Indira is India.") On the radio and in the newspapers, Mrs. Gandhi often compared herself to Joan of Arc; in an article entitled "My Secret of Success," which appeared in a major Hindi magazine in 1975, she revealed that her success was due to her childhood ambition to grow up to be like Joan of Arc. She was also fond of telling a story about her early involvement in the freedom struggle. When she was five, she recounted, she discovered that her doll was made in Britain. For days she pondered what she should do about it, and she struggled, in her words, "between love of the doll—[along with] pride in the ownership of such a lovely thing—and . . . duty towards my country." She continued, "At last the decision was made and, quivering with tension, I took the doll up on the roof terrace and set fire to her. Then the tears came as if they could never stop. And for some days I was ill with a temperature! To this day I hate striking a match!"

Under the Emergency, Mrs. Gandhi, who had always kept her own counsel, came to spend her off-duty hours almost entirely with her immediate family. She had no close friends. Rajiv and his wife (a native of Italy) and their two children lived with her, and so did Sanjay and Menaka. Sanjay also sat at her Emergency council meetings and served as her surrogate at meetings with petitioning politicians and officials. He attended all the Supreme Court sessions on her appeal, and was regularly seen at her side in public.

Sanjay, a short, slender, handsome man with curly black hair who dresses simply, in Indian clothes, first came to public notice in 1970, shortly after Mrs. Gandhi's government granted him the license, over the heads of established engineering firms and industrial groups, to build his factory to mass-produce the Maruti, named after the son of a Hindu wind god. (All major industry in India is licensed, ostensibly to make the best use of available raw materials.) Almost from the outset of the project, he and the Maruti became the center of political uproar. Charges of nepotism, of creating a government-sponsored monopoly, of accumulating wealth at the expense of the public, and of questionable financial dealings dogged him. At one time, one-fifth of the members of Parliament submitted a memorandum to Mrs. Gandhi demanding an investigation, but she dismissed the memorandum out of hand, as she had dismissed every attack on her son in Parliament or in the press. She announced in 1975, though, that all charges had been investigated and found groundless. It was said that in the meantime Sanjay had become rich. (During the Emergency, Sanjay's company branched out into other, more profitable ventures, serving, for instance, as agent for such foreign concerns as International Harvester and Demag, and marketing trucks, road rollers, cranes, and aircraft. Production of the

Maruti car was all but forgotten in the scramble for big foreign commissions and easily obtained government licenses.)

Reports about the relations between mother and son were so conflicting and implausible that it was hard to know what to make of them. For instance, Lewis Simons, of the Washington *Post,* who was perhaps the best foreign correspondent in India until he was expelled under the Emergency measures, wrote in the summer of 1975, "A family friend who attended a dinner party with Sanjay and Mrs. Gandhi several months ago said he saw the son slap his mother across the face 'six times.' 'She didn't do a thing,' the friend said. 'She just stood there and took it. She's scared to death of him.' " Yet Simons had also reported that when Mrs. Gandhi returned home after learning of her conviction, Sanjay "threw his arms around her and cried like a baby." On these statements, another family friend commented, "Not even a god could slap Mrs. Gandhi across the face six times. I know from an eyewitness that Sanjay only slapped her once. And as for Sanjay crying—he's a tough fellow and he doesn't cry."

Sanjay received his first official political commission in December of 1975: he was made a member of the executive committee of the youth wing of the Congress Party. During Nehru's Prime Ministership, it had been a parlor game to guess who would succeed him, and at one time or another various Congress leaders had been put forward as candidates. During Mrs. Gandhi's Prime Ministership, or, at least, following the proclamation of the Emergency, everyone took it for granted that Sanjay would succeed his mother. "The Prime Minister has undoubtedly endorsed her son's arrogation of power, much as her father encouraged her own early political career," *The Economist* noted in 1976. "Amateur psychologists in India offer two plausible explanations for this phenomenon: the classic suspiciousness of a dictator who ends up trusting only family and family retainers; the equally classic guilt of a working mother and single parent who overcompensates by bestowing gifts." Some psychologists also offered a third: the all-embracing love of a traditional Hindu mother, in whose eyes a son can do no wrong. But the political explanation for Sanjay's ascendancy could lie in his ruthless counsel to his mother to proclaim the Emergency. Interestingly, his ascendancy coincided with the arrest of Jaya Prakash Narayan, Mrs. Gandhi's spiritual father.

Before long, a personality cult grew up around Mrs. Gandhi and Sanjay. In the first nine months of the Emergency, a hundred and eighty documentary films were made about her and the Twenty-Point Program. (In one of the films, she was asked by a reporter why she thought no one ever tried to push her around, and she replied, "Well, because they know that— I mean, it has no effect, so they can waste their breath if they want to.") During the Emergency, Sanjay began to be compared to the sun, the moon, "the rising orbs." In the early months of the Emergency, the newspapers gave him a lot of front-page space, reporting on his whirlwind tours of the states—his receptions at airports by chief ministers, his walks through slums, his work for flood relief in Bihar. And his activities were not only featured on the front pages but also hailed by full-page advertisements inside, which had been placed by private firms seeking favors from the government. Later, there was a short time during which his activities were played down: discreet stories would appear on the inside pages—reporting, say, that a canal had been named after him, or that his supporters in the state of Uttar Pradesh had urged him to stand for Parliament, proclaiming him "Messiah Sanjay." Some mother-and-son-watchers, to whom Sanjay had become something of a devil figure, said that Mrs. Gandhi had cut him down to size because he wanted to move much faster politically than she was ready for him to; others said that he was receiving too much exposure and so was in danger of becoming a scapegoat for the Emergency; still others said that Mrs. Gandhi simply wanted to build up Sanjay slowly, and so, with his assumption of power, his work had become more routine.

Whatever the truth, important differences of both style and substance existed between mother and son. She was a socialist, even a pro-Communist; he was a conservative and a pro-capitalist. She continued to talk as if she would like to restore democracy someday; he seemed to have no patience with it. Her constituency was made up of a loose alliance of the poor, the civil servants, and the intelligentsia, many of whom had not ceased to see in her the hope of attaining socialist goals; his constituency was made up of big and small businessmen, who wanted to get rich while helping with the modernization of the country. She had her Twenty-Point Program, which bore some resemblance to the old five-year plans; he gave himself over to a Four-Point Program—the control of population growth, the beautification of the country, the extension of literacy, and the abolition of the dowry—which he recommended to the young and eager, presenting it as within the means of anyone, however small or powerless, and which had about it the air of the princely do-gooder. (He also identified himself with the abolition of the caste system.) Whereas her twenty points were expressed in officialese, his four points were expressed in slogans: "Plan Your Family," "One Man, One Tree," "Each One Teach One," and "Marry Without Dowry." In Connaught Circus, where Mrs. Gandhi had a sixty-foot billboard to advertise her twenty points, he had a ten-foot billboard to advertise his four points. Sanjay, moreover, was seen by some as a symbol of the youth of the Congress Party—as a symbol that the Congress was committed not to any one ideology of the right or left but only to social and economic progress. He himself let it be known that he thought the country should be governed by the young, or, at least, by people under fifty. (At the time, his mother was fifty-nine.) There came to be two power centers—Mrs. Gandhi's official Cabinet and Sanjay's kitchen Cabinet. One was made up of Party leaders, the other of Sanjay's freewheeling friends, most of them Punjabis, notorious for their tough, aggressive ways, and some of them relatives of his Punjabi wife. Until the Emergency, Mrs. Gandhi had relied for advice primarily on half a dozen high-caste, smooth-talking Brahmans from Kashmir—the homeland of the Nehrus. It was they who were dubbed by the English-language newspapers "the Kashmiri Mafia." Subsequently, they were mostly replaced by Sanjay's rough-and-ready "Punjabi Mafia." Sanjay's Chef de Cabinet, a Punjabi named Bansi Lal, modelled himself on Pratap Singh Khairon, a former autocratic chief minister of the Punjab, whom the same papers called "the Al Capone of Indian politics," and who met his death through assassination. In 1969, Bansi Lal, as chief minister of Haryana, a state bordering on Delhi, helped Sanjay get, much below the market value, a two-hundred-and-ninety-acre tract of prime farmland by expropriating it from farmers and the military. He very soon became one of Sanjay's closest friends, and in December of 1975 he was made Mrs. Gandhi's Minister of Defense. The inner circles of mother and son came to overlap considerably. In addition to Bansi Lal, they included a former member of the Prime Minister's Secretariat, Yashpal Kapoor, whose political work in Allahabad had been the basis for the judgment against Mrs. Gandhi; R. K. Dhavan, Kapoor's cousin; and Mohammad Yunus, a lifelong family friend. Sanjay, through his relationship with Bansi Lal, tried at one point to ingratiate himself with the Army, which, however, resisted his efforts. (Sanjay had more luck with the civil service, especially after a few civil servants who did not go along with his directives were transferred or were given early retirement.)

In August, 1976, Sanjay was the subject of a cover story in the Independence Day issue of the English-language *Illustrated Weekly,* the magazine most widely read by India's middle class. Khushwant Singh, the elder statesman of Indian journalism who was its editor, wrote the story, in which Sanjay was touted as one who had "roused the conscience of young people" and "injected a sense of urgency" and "shown how coils of red tape can be untangled." Singh went on to note that "though he has come to be feared and hated by some, he is looked up to by the vast majority of the people as the hope of the future." Singh's physical description of Sanjay was equally flattering. He credited Sanjay with fair skin—a coveted attribute—and dark, "fiercely intense and honest eyes." Singh observed, "Despite the receding hairline he is an incredibly handsome young man," and continued, "A faint smile hovers about his lips, but you can never be sure whether he is amused or bored, pleased or irritated." Sanjay was also presented as shy, withdrawn, and careful. The article was accompanied by a horoscope predicting for Sanjay the Prime Ministership, dangerous women, and an ascetic retirement, and there were illustrations with fulsome captions. (One caption described rather fantastically how, thanks to Sanjay, seven hundred and fifty thousand former Delhi slum dwellers at last lived like human beings—in new colonies, with roads, parks, banks, and community television sets.)

Singh was at pains to point out that although he interviewed Sanjay for more than two hours, Sanjay managed to elude him; it may be that inadvertently Singh so exposed the character of his subject that he felt the need to protect himself.

Singh asked Sanjay when he started taking an interest in politics.

"When? I can't remember exactly when, but in the atmosphere in which I was brought up it was hardly possible not to take an interest in politics," he replied. Singh wrote, "He waved his hands in space to emphasize what he meant. I could feel the presence of the spirits of his great-grandfather Motilal, his grandfather Jawaharlal, and his father, Feroze Gandhi. From the neighboring room I occasionally heard a feminine voice and imagined it must be that of his mother, Prime Minister Indira Gandhi. I realized it was a silly question to ask. Sanjay must have sipped politics from his feeding bottle."

Singh, however, went on to ask how Sanjay had come to know so many politicians and their views.

"For years they attacked me over Maruti," Sanjay replied. "The rest I got to know like everyone else does: through newspapers and what people were saying about them."

The interview continued:

"Do you remember much of your grandfather? . . . Were you close to him?"

"As close as other people are to their grandfathers."

"Did he influence your thinking in any way?"

"I cannot recall any specific way in which he influenced me."

"What about your father? Were you close to him?"

"Yes—like any son is to his father."

"Did he spend much time with you? Did he help you with your studies?"

"Yes, he helped me with my lessons."

"I suppose it is the same with your mother and your brother?"

"Yes, my relationship is no different than that of anyone else with his mother or brother." . . .

"Did you have a religious upbringing? Have you any views on religion?"

"No, I am not particularly religious. But I am not anti-religious either. . . ."

"What about books? Any book influenced you particularly?"

"I cannot think of any."

"What is your favorite reading? Poetry? Fiction? History? Biography?"

He smiled. "No, none of those." . . .

Once again I returned to politics, and asked, "You have done so much work of slum clearance in Delhi, why have you not tackled Bombay as yet?"

He smiled and shrugged his shoulders.

Reading the interview, one got the impression that Singh was full of good will, and wanted his subject to perform well. Singh was patient and unflappable. He had another go at Sanjay, still trying to draw him out:

I came out bluntly: "Why don't you stand for the Presidentship of the Congress?"

He laughed. "It is ridiculous. The question does not arise of my ever entertaining the idea."

"Is the Congress Party functioning to your satisfaction? Do you think it needs to be revitalized?" I probed.

"Oh, yes. The Congress needs a lot of revitalizing."

"Why don't you come in and do something about it?" I asked.

"The work of the Youth Congress is more than enough for me."

"Your earlier statements, especially in the magazine *Surge,* were reassuring to a large section of people who were afraid of the extreme leftists getting a greater hold in the [Congress Party]. They seem to feel that of late you have been silent on these issues. What is the reason?"

"I have not changed my views on anything. . . ."

"What do you feel about the proposed amendments to the Constitution?"

"I don't know enough about the Constitution."

"Do you read the *Weekly?*"

"Only the jokes and comics. . . ."

"What is your interest? Politics?"

"I consider politics very boring. Most magazines that write on politics are uninteresting and dull."

Singh did not pursue the question of whether or not Sanjay was actually interested in politics, and the article went on to give us these biographical details: Sanjay was born at 9:27 A.M. on December 14, 1946; a Sagittarian, he shared his birthday with the idol of the masses, the film actor Raj Kapoor. A woman, Vimla Sindhi, who used to keep an eye on him when he was a toddler, had become the deputy director of the Hospitality Section of the Ministry of External Affairs. He attended a kindergarten, on the fashionable Curzon Road in Delhi, that was run by Elizabeth Gauba, a German-born woman who was married to an Indian. She remembered Sanjay as a boy of average intelligence, yet one possessing the self-confidence of a member of the Nehru family, and recalled that he preferred the company of animals to that of human beings. He next attended an elementary school in Mussoorie—a secluded hill station in Uttar Pradesh—and then the sprawling Doon School, in nearby Dehra Dun, which charged such high fees that only the very rich could afford to send their sons there. One of his Doon School friends, Gautam Vohra (who became an assistant editor of the *Times of India*), recalled, "Sanjay was not a very serious student. He used to sit next to me in the last row for the English period. We were studying some fascinating books, such as 'Lorna Doone' and 'Hajji Baba of Ispahan.' But they did not appear to inspire Sanjay. He did not take much interest in team sports, either. Winning one's colors in cricket, hockey, or football, or the gold badge was one way of gaining seniority and being made a house monitor or a school prefect. Sanjay did not seem interested in such positions." (Sanjay was also disruptive, sent down from Doon School for being "uncontrollable.") An old family friend noted that Sanjay never developed bad habits, like smoking or drinking, and abstained from coffee and tea. Another friend, after remarking that the word "fear" was not in Sanjay's vocabulary, recalled, "One day he came in a secondhand Land-Rover and asked me to accompany him, as he wanted to test the brakes. He took the car to a steep hillock . . . and just let it come down. Luckily, the brakes worked, or I wouldn't be here today." In fact, Sanjay's only interest in life at that time, apparently, was cars—how they were put together and how they worked. He went to Great Britain and served as an apprentice for three years in the Rolls-Royce plant. (He apparently failed his training course.) He returned home with his dream of the Maruti, and shortly received his government license to build the car and obtained the backing of rich industrialists. (Sanjay continued to devote part of his time to the production of the Maruti—some demonstration models were built, and proved faulty, though a few were sighted on the streets—even as he worked for the Four-Point Program and with the Youth Congress.) His wife, the "lanky Sikh beauty" Menaka, was a daughter of Colonel T. S. Anand and a granddaughter of the late Sir Datar Singh, who was a cattle breeder and one of the biggest zamindars in the British Punjab. (Under the Emergency, Menaka rediscovered her passion for journalism and floated a publishing house to bring out two monthly magazines, one of which, *Surya,* was an imitation of the color supplements in the London Sunday papers, to be carried by Indian newspapers. Menaka followed the old

Congress Party technique of financing publications by cajoling friends and businessmen to advertise, and it was said that *Surya* was almost at once completely booked with advertisements for three years. Menaka named herself managing editor, with a salary of five thousand rupees a month, and named her mother managing director.)

"Sanjay Gandhi has many more critics than his mother," Singh concluded. " 'On whose authority is Sanjay doing what he is doing?' they ask. . . . Why cavil about someone who is at long last getting [something] done? Sanjay has taken a heavy load on his young shoulders. He has a long and arduous road ahead of him. Do not strew banana skins on his path. Help him to reach his goal of a prosperous and happy India. We, of the older generation, can only dream dreams. Let our young men see visions and make those visions a reality."

Khushwant Singh was such an enthusiastic supporter of the Gandhi family and the Emergency that he was popularly dubbed Khushamad, or Flatterer, Singh. He was certainly adept at picking his way among the land mines then scattered in the journalist's field. While frequently featuring mother and son in the *Weekly's* pages, he managed to give an illusion of journalistic independence. Indeed, this Sanjay story was followed by a defense of nonviolent agitation by one of Mahatma Gandhi's leading disciples, J. B. Kripalani, who argued that true nonviolent agitation could never be confused with lawlessness and anarchy, since men like Socrates and Gandhi—and, by implication, Jaya Prakash Narayan—had such respect for the law that they cheerfully accepted the legal penalty for their disobedience, even if it was life imprisonment or death.

# 6

## Prisoners
## of Conscience

"It is with a heavy, sorrow-stricken heart that I am writing this, further to my letter dated May 12, 1976 . . . with the hope of obtaining justice at your hands," wrote Mrs. Alice Fernandes to the President of India on May 24, 1976, in a letter that became widely circulated abroad. "I am an old lady of sixty-five years, and my seventy-five-year-old husband is a heart patient. The recent events narrated hereunder have left us terribly shaken and grief-stricken." She went on to say that around nine o'clock on the evening of May 1st the police arrived at her home, in the city of Bangalore, and took her second son, Lawrence, into custody. They interrogated him until three o'clock in the morning concerning the whereabouts of his elder brother, George. Lawrence apparently insisted that he had no idea where his brother was, and they began torturing him. They beat him with a club. It broke. They beat him with another club. It, too, broke. They went through five clubs. Then they whipped him with the root of a banyan tree. They kicked him and slapped him around. He still denied any knowledge of George's whereabouts. They threatened to throw him under a moving train.

Lawrence's brother George, chairman of the Socialist Party, was one of the most notorious members of the opposition. He was a leader of the million-strong railway workers' union. He had organized the 1974 railway strike and was one of the thousands of workers Mrs. Gandhi had arrested. (The assassination, on January 3, 1975, of Lalit Narayan Mishra, Minister of Railways, and one of the most important and controversial members of Mrs. Gandhi's Cabinet—he was the first national figure to be assassinated since Mahatma Gandhi, in 1948—has been attributed in part to his ruthless and arbitrary exercise of power during the strike, though who the assassins were and what their motives may have been is still a subject of dispute.) George had been released, but at the onset of the Emergency he had gone underground. The government contended that since then he and twenty-four other defendants had conspired to blow up several public buildings and sections of railway tracks in different parts of the country and had incited people to violently overthrow their government. A nationwide search for him had been going on for nearly a year, but he had evaded capture. Moreover, he had given interviews from his hideouts to the international press, attacking Mrs. Gandhi and the Emergency and claiming that people throughout the country were with him and were protecting him. ("It has been my constant appeal to the people in the North to get rid of this dictatorship if they want to preserve the unity of the country, because a situation is bound to arise where people from the South are going to say that we are part of a democratic India, we are not a part of an India that is ruled by a dictator from Kashmir.") By being at large, he was an embarrassment to the government and an advertisement of its ineptitude.

Mrs. Fernandes, in her letter, asserted that the government was persecuting her family in the hope of getting at her son George. Lawrence was kept in solitary confinement and given no food for three days. When he became unconscious, he was taken from hospital to hospital for treatment, but under a false name to conceal his identity. After three weeks of searching for him, the mother was admitted to her son's cell. She found him "looking dead." He had lost considerable weight. His left side was paralyzed, his left hand and leg were swollen. He talked falteringly, and he was so nervous that he would start at the sound of approaching feet or at the sight of a khaki uniform. He required the help of two people to move at all. Yet Mrs. Fernandes claimed in her letter that neither he nor anyone else in the family knew the whereabouts of George Fernandes. "Whatever I have stated here is on the basis of what the family could gather from Lawrence during the visits to him in the cell," the letter went on. "I urge upon you in the name of all that is good in civilized conduct of human beings and their governments and in the name of justice to order a thorough judicial enquiry into this barbaric torture etc. and take suitable action against the concerned authorities."

In June, 1976, soon after Mrs. Fernandes sent her letter, George Fernandes was apprehended in Calcutta. His wife, Leila Kabir Fernandes, who had gone to America a few months earlier, sent a cablegram to Mrs. Gandhi inquiring after her husband and protesting Lawrence's ordeal. A few days later, she received this reply from the Ministry of Home Affairs, in New Delhi: "Your telegram of 17th June inquiring about George Fernandes. How can you not be aware of the activities of your husband, who has for the past several months been moving about instigating people to commit acts of violence, subversion, sabotage, and other serious crimes prejudicial to public order and security of the country? He was arrested in Calcutta on 10th June and is in legal custody in connection with several criminal cases under investigation. He is in his normal health. Allegation of torture of his brother Lawrence Fernandes is totally false, baseless, and mischievous."

Possibly because of the international interest in George Fernandes' case—his wife later toured Europe to publicize his plight and that of his brother, who was apparently still in jail—Mrs. Gandhi decided to put him on public trial. In fact, he and the Anand Marg leader, Prabhat Ranjan Sarkar, became the first major opposition figures to be put on trial during the Emergency.

From June 26, 1975, when citizens in many parts of India were suddenly awakened by the police in the middle of the night and carted off to jails without a charge or a warrant, until January 18, 1977, when new elections were announced, the series of knock-on-the-door arrests continued, in keeping with a prolonged campaign to stamp out all dissent. In May, 1976, Mrs. Gandhi's Home Affairs Ministry disclosed that the number of people it had arrested solely for printing and disseminating underground broadsheets came to seven thousand. The officials insisted, however, that many of the prisoners were not Mrs. Gandhi's political opponents ("prisoners of conscience") but, rather, hoarders and black marketeers ("anti-social elements" or "bad elements") who had previously been able to exploit constitutional guarantees against such arrests to escape prosecution. Even so, the officials refused to release any information about the prisoners—their identities, the sites and conditions of their jails, the state of their health, the length of their imprisonment—claiming that it was all a "state secret;" they forbade families of the prisoners to inquire about them, newspapers to publish their names, and courts to conduct hearings or trials, or even to entertain writs of habeas corpus. Moreover, according to Mrs. Gandhi's acting Home Affairs Minister, Om Mehta, "in the case of persons whose detention is declared to be necessary for effectively dealing with the Emergency, the grounds of detention shall be treated as confidential matters of state whose disclosure will be against the public interest, and shall not be communicated to the person detained." There were constant reports of torture and mistreatment of the political prisoners, and Amnesty International and other independent bodies made repeated requests for an investigation of such reports, but Mrs. Gandhi's government refused to accede to these, or even permit anyone to see or interview the political prisoners. "Here Mrs. Gandhi's regime shows itself even less responsive to the principles of human rights than many other police states, such as Chile, Taiwan, the Soviet Union, Indonesia, and South Korea," the late Ivan Morris, chairman of the American branch of Amnesty International, noted in a letter to the *Times*.

There was much speculation about the number of the political prisoners—estimates at the time varying from thirty thousand to two hundred and fifty thousand. In 1976, on being asked to divulge the number, Mrs. Gandhi said, "It's a small number of people, very small, relative to India's whole population"—as if because the prison population was a small fraction of the total population it were of no consequence, and as if there were some direct relation between the two numbers.

Mrs. Gandhi's use of sweeping emergency powers had a long line of precedents in Indian history. Nehru's government invoked the authority of the British Defense of India Rules during the 1962 Sino-Indian War to peremptorily arrest many Communist leaders. Mrs. Gandhi's own government, during the "emergency" of the 1967–68 guerrilla warfare in Nagaland and the Mizo Hills, on the northeastern frontier, "pacified" entire villages by turning them into makeshift military prisons.

But all along, and especially since independence, questions had been raised in India about the morality and the legality of the use of such emergency powers: How could the suspension of all civil liberties and human rights ever be justified in a democratic society? And if it was ever justifiable, how was the government to determine that an emergency necessitating it really existed? As long as the Indian government used its emergency powers against small sections of society—the Communists, the Nagas, the Mizos—such questions were mostly ignored. But during the emergency proclaimed in June of 1975 these powers were used in such a wholesale manner that the following winter the Supreme Court of India itself was asked to address the questions. In seven state High Courts, the government had been the defendant in habeas-corpus cases brought by forty-three political prisoners, including four members of Parliament, and it had lost all of them. In its appeal to the Supreme Court, the government contended that it had proclaimed the Emergency under the emergency provisions of the constitution, and that citizens' rights guaranteed under any other part of the constitution—such as the rights to life and liberty, the right to equality before the law, and the right of habeas corpus—could consequently be suspended. The political prisoners contended that such rights were so "fundamental" that they were rooted in "the rule of law" and could not be suspended by any procedural provisions of the constitution.

On April 28, 1976, the Supreme Court upheld the government's position, by a vote of four to one. The case was decided on two narrow legal issues: whether the political prisoners could file writs of habeas corpus during the Emergency, and, if so, what the extent of the judicial scrutiny of the government's grounds for their arrests should be. Chief Justice Ray wrote one of the majority opinions. "Liberty is confined and controlled by law," he wrote. "It is not an absolute freedom. If extraordinary powers are given [by the constitution], they are given because the emergency is extraordinary." Ray held that neither the political prisoners nor the courts need be apprised of the government's grounds for the arrests: "Material and information on which orders of preventive detention are passed necessarily belong to a class of documents whose disclosure would impair the proper functioning of public service and administration. The file relating to a detention order must contain intelligence reports whose confidentiality is beyond reasonable question."

In a concurring opinion, Justice Y. V. Chandrachud said that courts of law could not look upon the Emergency with any mental reservations: "Judge and jury alike may form their personal assessment of a political situation but whether the emergency should be declared or not is a matter of high state policy, and questions of policy are impossible to examine in courts of law."

Justice M. H. Beg, in his concurring opinion, drew an analogy between governments and parents: "The constitutional duty of every government faced with threats of widespread disorder and chaos . . . cannot be denied. . . . Even parents have to take appropriate preventive action against those children who may threaten to burn down the house they live in."

The lone dissenting opinion was written by Justice H. R. Khanna, who, invoking the tradition of Plato, the Magna Carta, and the American Declaration of Independence, wrote, "The power of the courts to issue a writ of habeas corpus is regarded as one of the most important characteristics of democratic states under the rule of law. The principle that no one shall be deprived of his liberty without the authority of law was not the gift of the constitution. It existed before the coming into force of the constitution." Khanna pointed out that without court protection any capricious or malicious petty official could arrest any persons, or even whole families, and keep them in prison indefinitely. Such officials would not even have the need to conjure up the spectre of public disorder or of a threat to national security, and, since they would not be answerable to any law or court, they would wield despotic powers. Khanna wrote, "Whether such things actually come to pass is not the question before us: it is enough to state that these are permissible consequences from the acceptance of the contention that [the constitution] is the sole repository of the right to life and personal liberty and that consequent upon the issue of the Presidential Order [proclaiming a national emergency] no one can approach any court and seek relief during the period of the emergency against deprivation of life or personal liberty." He noted, "In a purely formal sense, even the organized mass murders of the Nazi regime qualify as law."

The effect of the majority opinions, however, was that the government had to be accepted as acting in good faith. (The dissenting opinion was a feat of temerity, since all the judges lived and worked under the threat of arrest, and were certainly mindful of the fact that dissident members of Parliament were among the first persons to be arrested. Khanna was not arrested, but when, on January 29, 1977, Ray retired as Chief Justice, Mrs. Gandhi reached over the head of Khanna, the most senior justice, and appointed Beg.) But critics out of the reach of the government found little reason to credit it with good faith. In Birmingham, England, on August 10, 1975—six weeks after the proclamation of the Emergency, and eight and a half months before the Supreme Court's disposal of the case—a young woman named Mary Tyler addressed the Indian Workers' Association, an organization of Indians living in Britain, on the theme of political prisoners in India. She was a British subject who had lived in India and was married to an Indian who had been imprisoned on the suspicion that he was a Naxalite. As a result of her marriage, she was also suspected of being a Naxalite and spent five years, from 1970 to 1975, as a political prisoner in Indian jails, most of the time in the Hazaribagh Central Jail, in Bihar. Her remarks were later published in the *New India Bulletin*, a Canadian Marxist publication of the Indian People's Association in North America, and in 1976 they became the basis of a book she wrote, entitled "My Years in an Indian Prison." Miss Tyler said in her remarks that everyone was always asking, "How *many* political prisoners are there in India?" She said that she did not have the slightest idea, and that the numbers did not really matter; but she recalled that when she was in Hazaribagh Central Jail there were from two hundred to three hundred prisoners like her, whom the government had branded "Naxalites." Many of them were indeed known to be Naxalites, but others were merely suspected of being members of the movement. Moreover, other kinds of political prisoners were always turning up. Sometimes they were demonstrators—students, lawyers, intellectuals—but more often than not they were striking railway workers, striking teachers, or striking hospital workers. As soon as a demonstration was crushed or a strike broken, such political prisoners were released, but she estimated that at one time—at the height of Jaya Prakash Narayan's political agitation in Bihar in 1974—there were as many as six thousand political prisoners in the Hazaribagh Central Jail. As a rule, the "Naxalites" were never released, and were singled out for the worst prison treatment. Most were crowded into small, dingy cells—sometimes five to a cell. There was not so much as a fan, and the only light was from a naked electric bulb overhead, which was left burning all night. The only ventilation was through the bars of the doors. The "Naxalite" prisoners were denied decent sanitary facilities, adequate diet, adequate clothing, and even adequate drinking water, and at times were denied any exercise. (What made Miss Tyler's testimony remarkably convincing was that although she said much about the suffering of the others, she said hardly anything about her own. She merely noted in passing that she owed her eventual release to being a foreigner.) Some of the "Naxalite" prisoners were kept in solitary confinement, without books or newspapers. The political prisoners were allowed visitors only in rare instances, and almost their only outside contact was through censored letters, delivered long after they were written. "Naxalites" were kept shackled in bar fetters—an apparatus of iron rods and rings—which weighed about nine pounds, and which made it all but impossible for them to walk, sit, squat, sleep, or even use the lavatory in an ordinary way. The fetters were put on the "Naxalites" the moment they entered the prison, and were thereafter kept on them night and day, in cold weather and hot. (Bihar is hot much of the year.) The fetters caused running sores, and left many of the prisoners disabled or deformed. "I cannot precisely say how many people are in fetters at a single time," Miss Tyler observed. "Often the prisoners are able to get these fetters removed after hunger strikes and other protests, but they are hardly out of fetters for more than 15 days at a time when the jail authorities put them back on them on the flimsiest excuse." Flies and mosquitoes proliferated. A great many of the prisoners came down with malaria, filariasis, typhoid, smallpox, tuberculosis, leprosy. Some were beaten and tortured, and occasionally one was shot. They had no recourse from the arbitrary punishment of their jailers and no chance of release either on bail or on compassionate or medical grounds.

Of course, in those days the government was legally obliged to prefer charges and issue warrants; a political prisoner could demand a writ of habeas corpus and a court hearing, and could carry his petition all the way to the Supreme Court and perhaps win release. Even if he was rearrested immediately thereafter— as political prisoners often were—he could at least support himself with hope in his prison cell.

As the Emergency continued, the catalogue of Indian acts of brutality, based on eyewitness reports from those imprisoned during the latest emergency—which were gathered by the International League for Human Rights and presented to the United Nations for action in June, 1976—included beating prisoners with steel rods and rifle butts, burning their skin with candles, tying rods to their necks to stretch their spinal cords, suspending them by their feet, inserting live electric wires in crevices of their bodies. To be sure, acts of brutality on this scale, however appalling, are unique neither to India nor to our times. But they have no precedent in the India of Indira Gandhi's father, or of his spiritual father, Mahatma Gandhi.

# 7

# Sterilization Campaign and Khichripur

One day in April of 1976, a number of vans and bulldozers assembled in front of the Muslim slum quarter near the Turkman Gate, in Old Delhi. Several elegantly dressed young women volunteers jumped down, rushed into the slum quarter, and started nabbing male slum dwellers or beggars who looked old enough to have three or more children and marching them off to a hastily set-up tent for vasectomies. Many other well-dressed volunteers, both men and women, descended from the vans into the slum and began rounding up the entire community, of some hundreds of residents, for transportation to new developments on the outskirts of the city, while the bulldozers positioned themselves to raze the place. The volunteers were members of a work party—one of many such parties laboring all over the city on behalf of Sanjay's Four-Point Program.

Because Sanjay lived in Delhi, the city had become the laboratory for his four points, and especially for his campaign for sterilization, which the authorities were heralding as the test of Mrs. Gandhi's "New India." Certainly no part of his Four-Point Program had created a greater stir in the political establishment than the launching of the sterilization campaign that spring. The central government had started drafting a bill for compulsory national sterilization of all men with more than three children, on pain of fine and imprisonment, and state governments had started legislating local programs. The three million government employees in Delhi had been led to believe that they might be deprived of their housing and pensions if they had families of more than three children and were not sterilized by October of 1977. Sidewalk sterilization clinics had sprung up all over the city, under bright-colored tents. The vasectomy, a five-minute, bloodless procedure, was being promoted as no more complicated than vaccination. The authorities would hustle men off the streets and into the tents, tempt them with a bonus—from sixty to a hundred and twenty rupees (from eight to sixteen dollars), a tin of cooking oil, or a clock—and sterilize them. They would send the sterilized men back onto the streets without a thought for the psychological implications of the operation. The drive for sterilization had reached such proportions that on a certain day the authorities informed all government schoolteachers that if they wished to collect their pay each of them would have to produce four slum dwellers for sterilization; another day a similar edict went out to the policemen. There was such pressure on government employees to produce candidates for sterilization, such a scramble for eligible slum dwellers, that they would draft the same beggars many times over and "sterilize" them. Some beggars would also go back on their own for additional bonuses. It was rumored that sometimes even young boys who had never been married and had no children were being dragged into the tents and sterilized. It was a mass program to solve a mass problem, and therefore the only thing that counted was the statistics.

As the volunteers went about their business in the Turkman Gate slum quarter that April day, the rumor spread that the Muslim poor were to be not only displaced and sterilized but made impotent (the operation was falsely thought to interfere with potency), and that Sanjay's Hindu acolytes were hauling in Muslim bachelors and bridegrooms for "the sacrilegious operation." By religious law, Muslims are allowed four wives. Nehru, Lal Bahadur Shastri, and Mrs. Gandhi herself had all been champions of minority rights and secularism, and so, although Hindus were required by civil law to be monogamous, Muslims were permitted, out of respect for their religious law, to be polygamous. But Sanjay had recently stated, in a much publicized pronouncement, that anyone who lived in India would have to be first a citizen of India and second a Muslim, Hindu, Sikh, Parsi, or whatever. Since Sanjay was known to be a man of action, his pronouncement had terrified the Muslims. As it happened, the launching of the sterilization campaign had coincided with the slum-clearance campaign—Sanjay's beautification program—and the coincidence had made Muslims fear that an anti-Muslim policy was being initiated.

Old men and Muslim priests now began running through the slum quarter shouting that Sanjay's troops had come to destroy the Muslims—raze their homes, take away their women, and transport the men to prison camps. "Throw the Hindu infidels back into the vans!" someone shouted. "Guard your women and children in the name of Allah, and defend your religion!" While women and children barricaded themselves in their huts, the men poured out in a mob. The mob seethed and snaked through the slum, hurling stones, bricks, and Molotov cocktails at the volunteers, their vans, their bulldozers, their clinic. The police quickly arrived, charged, and started firing into the crowd. But the rioting continued for many hours. Before the mob was dispersed, hundreds had been injured and at least fifty killed.

Ultimately, the slum dwellers—men, women, and children— were herded into the vans at gunpoint. Even as the vans started pulling out, the bulldozers began demolishing the huts behind them. The vans were driven across the Jumna and their occupants deposited on farmland that had been fenced off with barbed wire. Each slum family was given twenty-five square yards of land— piled up with bricks for building shelters—and was issued ration cards, which were good for buying rations only at a shop on the development site. Men with big families were told that if they did not get sterilized in the clinic on the development site within a prescribed time, their ration cards would not be renewed. Then the Muslims were left, angry and humiliated, to fend for themselves. It was the beginning of the Delhi summer—the season for epidemics.

A few days later, stories of the plight of the transplanted slum dwellers reached the ears of the Muslim leader Sheikh Mohammed Abdullah, in Kashmir, who, after spending many years in prison for fighting the Indian government, had capitulated and was now keeping the state safe and quiet for Mrs. Gandhi. To see the conditions for himself, he came to Delhi and went on a tour of the settlement—now called Khichripur. (Khichripur means "hodgepodge town"; the English word "kedgeree" is derived from the Hindi *khichri*.) So that the government could attend to any grievances immediately, he took along with him Mrs. Gandhi's closest family friend, Mohammad Yunus. Instead of finding in Khichripur the advertised community road, park, school, bank, and television of Sanjay's new developments, the Sheikh was confronted by a sprawling camp mired in mud and sludge, swarming with flies, and emitting a noxious stench. Men, women, and children, sick and disoriented, were living in crude, often uncovered shelters. When they learned who he was, they crowded around him.

Sheikh Abdullah told them that they could speak to him without fear of government reprisal—that Mohammad Yunus had come as a token of Mrs. Gandhi's personal concern. They unburdened themselves to the Sheikh. They wanted food and medicine. They had no mosque to pray in. The land was neither piped for water nor wired for electricity. There were no real prospects of any kind for shops and businesses. They hadn't as yet even seen the bus that was supposed to take them to their jobs in the city. Loans from the government for building new shelters were made conditional on the sacrilegious operation. The men were being forcibly dragged off to the sterilization clinic, and now the authorities had even begun performing a similar operation (tubectomy) on the women. How could Sheikh Sahib, a great Muslim leader, a faithful servant of Allah, let infidels do such terrible things to His people?

Sheikh Abdullah was so indignant that he asked Mohammad

Yunus to take him straight to Mrs. Gandhi. As they were getting into the car, parked at the edge of Khichripur, a woman came running up to them. "Police have started rounding up people!" she cried. "My husband has been taken!"

No one knows what occurred between Sheikh Abdullah and Mrs. Gandhi, but it was said that a social worker who had worked in the Turkman Gate slum quarter, and had complained directly to Sanjay about the manner of the uprooting, was made to spend a couple of nights in jail for "meddling."

Some months after the establishment of Khichripur, Mohammad Yunus remarked, "I am a classic example of the success of family planning. I am the forty-second child of my father, and I have only one child—a son." Rajni Kothari, at the time a visiting professor at Columbia University, wrote in the final Emergency issue of *Seminar*, "It was perhaps felt that one way of legitimizing the Emergency was to show some dramatic results and the one area where this could be done was population control. This understanding was quickly seen by some as a green signal for using all kinds of measures to force the people—mostly the vulnerable sections among them—and show results." Often the burden of this campaign fell on slum dwellers and Untouchables, who, being the poorest of the poor, were the most vulnerable and also the easiest to round up, and on government employees, who were the easiest to coerce and, being the best off as a class, had the most to lose by noncompliance. But after the Turkman Gate riot (one of many such violent outbreaks over sterilization across the country) Mrs. Gandhi had vigorously tried to dissociate herself from the bill for compulsory national sterilization. She began saying she believed that the government should first work on programs of incentives for maintaining small families, and refrain from attempts to force Muslims to be monogamous. But there was no such sign of moderation on the part of Sanjay. The state governments, caught between the conflicting stands of mother and son, could only equivocate on the issue—on the one hand, let it be known that there should not be any connection between family planning and religion, and, on the other, invoke Muhammad's injunction that marriage should be conditional upon the ability to support a family. In the meantime, there was apparently no letup in the campaign for "voluntary" sterilization. Between April and September of 1976 alone, two million people were sterilized. (In the previous two decades, sixteen million people had been sterilized.)

No one questions the urgency of controlling the population of India. Every year, there are thirteen million more babies, and since independence the population has nearly doubled. Many family-planning methods were tried before the Emergency, with little success. The villagers lacked the sense of calendar time needed for the rhythm method, and had no means to buy various kinds of contraceptives. When intrauterine devices were inserted free of charge, the women, most of whom were anemic, tended to have bleeding problems. Superstitions and fears concerning bleeding, together with a lack of medical followup, defeated that method, too. Sterilization also failed then, in part because it was voluntary and was restricted to cities with medical facilities. In any event, under the democratic system there was no way of forcing birth control upon people who regarded children, especially sons, as helping hands and the only security for their old age. Then, under the Emergency, sterilization, whether technically voluntary or actually compulsory, was touted as the answer to India's prayers. But the campaign for sterilization was the first Emergency measure to affect rich and poor alike, and, in their different ways, they mobilized against it. Consequently, the campaign threatened to undo what little progress had been made in family planning; indeed, it might hopelessly discredit the concept of family planning with the Indian people as a whole, for, in the words of Kothari, "it created an atmosphere of shock and disbelief, producing severe backlash." Moreover, recent demographic research suggests, paradoxically, that, whatever family-planning methods are used in an underdeveloped country, it may be that there can be no significant decline in the country's population until there is a significant decline in the high mortality rate, which encourages people to try to have large families. And the high mortality rate is a consequence of ignorance and poverty. Today, one of every four Indian children dies before the age of five, less often from the old killers like malaria, cholera, smallpox, and tuberculosis than from infections like tetanus; in the Punjab alone, according to one estimate, as many as a third of the neonatal deaths are still the result of a village midwife's unhygienic cutting of the umbilical cord. It may be, therefore, that there can be no significant decline in the high mortality rate until there is a significant diffusion of education and the benefits of economic development.

# 8

# The Bangladesh
# Pattern

Soon after the Emergency was proclaimed, one member of the
Congress Party, Krishnan Kant, made an eloquent and wide-
ranging indictment of it—a sort of *cri de coeur*—in what could
properly be called the rump Parliament, inasmuch as so many of
both its opposition and its Congress members had been jailed.
Kant was forthwith expelled from the Party. He rejected the
whole rationale of the Emergency, saying that the people who
were so loud in support of it as a quick and easy answer to India's
social and economic needs, and were decrying democratic institutions and civil liberties as bourgeois luxuries ill-suited to a poor
country, were the very people who had been amassing wealth at
the expense of the poor and sabotaging all efforts at reform ever
since independence, and that the Congress Party leaders who
were being punished for misconduct by expulsion or arrest were
not those saboteurs but people who had attacked corruption in
the Party and insisted on the Party's living up to the letter and
spirit of its promises. He went on to say that whenever, in independent India, industries were in fact nationalized, as had been
promised, it was the former owners rather than the workers who
benefitted; that, similarly, whenever a piece of land-reform legislation was passed, as had been promised, it was so full of loop-
holes that the landowners kept their land and the landless peasants

remained landless; that even when, after the 1972 drought, the government took over the distribution of wheat expressly to prevent hoarders and black marketeers from profiting by the widespread hunger of their countrymen, many of the government officials and Congress men and women involved became hoarders and black marketeers themselves. These, Kant said, were the very people who, after Jaya Prakash Narayan came along with his protest movement, closed ranks and instituted the Emergency, engulfing the country in a great political silence and enveloping it in a thick fog so that they could continue their nefarious activities unchecked and unchallenged. With their new dictatorial powers, they were able to force down prices, to force up production in factories, to enforce discipline in schools and universities, and also to dismiss a few incompetent government officials and to make the trains run on time—in short, to make the Emergency popular, and thus better conceal the fact that the old concentration of property and privilege remained undisturbed. Kant noted that "after the imposition of Emergency the government has suspended Articles 19, 20, and 21, regarding fundamental rights of freedom of speech and expression and personal liberty, but not Article 31, relating to right of property," and went on, "No privileges of the privileged classes are being touched. They have been reassured. There is going to be no nationalization of textile and sugar industries. . . . On the other hand, the Emergency will come down on the workers, on students, the intelligentsia, and the fixed-income groups. I would like to ask my friends if this is really a swing to the left or whether it is not in fact a swing to the right?"

Kant, reiterating some of the unanswered criticisms of the Emergency, recalled that after its proclamation Mrs. Gandhi had said that in a country as vast and diverse as India no dictatorship could succeed—that its effect would only be to divide and Balkanize the country—yet she had also said repeatedly that the nation was greater than democracy. How could such contradictory statements be reconciled, Kant asked. Again, he recalled, she had said in defense of the Emergency that the number of persons she had arrested was an extremely small proportion of the Indian population. And yet she must have known that the very climate of emergency, the very fear of peremptory arrest, created a most unhealthy political atmosphere, conducive only to conspiratorial politics. In such desperate circumstances, he continued, the people to fear were not the men and women who were now in jail, since they believed in open society and open politics—as Nehru used to say, worked in the sun and in the light—but the terrorists and the palace guards who were now at large, since they believed in secret, furtive politics and hatched their plots in the darkness of night. The palace guards might be even more sinister and dangerous than the terrorists, because, being sycophants, rank opportunists, time servers, and unprincipled men, they were ruled only by ambition and vied with each other to pronounce their loyalty to whoever happened to sit on the throne at a particular time. It was therefore in Mrs. Gandhi's own interest to try to settle her differences with her opponents through dialogue and accommodation rather than through emergency and repression. But the counsels of reason had been drowned out by the din and the machinations of those people with vested interests. Who now dared to attack the government's failures and to expose the people with vested interests, Kant asked. They had seen to it that there was no freedom of speech, because they thought any criticism of government policy was a criticism of them. Kant also said:

> A free press is the greatest strength of an efficient democratic system. When you stifle the flow of information to the people in this country, you are blocking the channel of information to yourself. . . . You are not going to increase the efficiency of the system. Rather, you are robbing it of any efficiency it might have had. We have heard Mussolini—for the first time—ran trains on time in Italy. We have heard of Ayub Khan bringing down the prices [after his military coup in Pakistan in 1958]. Jawaharlal Nehru was not taken in by these gimmicks. He knew that these were not the ways of adding efficiency to the system. . . . Till now, if the right reactionaries and left adventurists have not been able to

launch on a path of violence in this country, it was mainly because of the open society. It was our greatest insurance. Now this emergency and the accompanying blackout gives them the cover they need to hatch conspiracies. Those who brought about this emergency know not what grievous harm they are doing to the nation and to themselves. . . .

We in this country have learnt at the feet of Gandhiji [Mahatma Gandhi] that ends and means are inseparable— rather, means are more important than ends. . . . When you resort to undemocratic and coercive methods, even with the best of intentions, they release forces . . . over which one has no control. The person releasing these forces becomes, inadvertently, or maybe innocently, a prisoner of such forces and [is] no more . . . a free agent. . . . Then a nation has to pay a very heavy price to save its soul.

I am not wedded to the Westminster model of democracy. I am prepared to look at various alternatives. But what we see happening before our eyes is, on the one hand, the hopeful dream of those who talk of a limited dictatorship becoming a nightmare of full dictatorship, and, on the other hand, the death of parties, resulting in a partyless system. . . . Any dictatorship which is not based on an ideology will not be the dictatorship of a leadership, will not be the dictatorship of a party or a class, but will become the tyranny of the constable, the clerk, and the petty official. Let us not be deluded by the sacking of a few petty officials. All this happened not once, twice, but thrice in Pakistan, when Ayub Khan took over, when Yahya Khan took over, and when [Zulfikar Ali] Bhutto took over.

The Indian freedom struggle has been a glowing saga in the world history. It blazed . . . a nonviolent path for the liberation of oppressed peoples. Many subject nations took inspiration from it. Gandhi and his ideology became a beacon light to Asian and African countries. Nehru tried to imbibe the spirit and establish the parliamentary system and lay the foundation of an open society. The whole freedom struggle was directed towards this end. It was because of the strong [tradition], and correct tendencies built up through fire and travails, that when many newly emergent countries of Asia and Africa, one after the other, fell under dictatorships, India stood as a great bastion of democracy and open society. . . . My pride and faith have received a rude shock when I find people recommending the throwing away of this precious legacy [in order to] follow the examples of other Asian and African countries . . . where freedom of press and right of dissent and the right to move in the court or the right to know the crime for which one is being punished—the very prerequisites of democracy—have been extinguished. If we are forced on this path, it would mean the negation of the last seventy-five years of Indian history. Would it not be as if Gandhi never trod this earth and the whole fight we waged for the propagation of high democratic principles was just a freak, unconnected with the past or the future?

Kant saw the Emergency as an aberrant departure from the tradition of "high democratic principles" which he celebrated. But it may be that the Emergency was the logical culmination of a process that had been at work in India—and, in fact, in the subcontinent as a whole—ever since independence. Of course, from the British days on, freedom and self-determination had been the great rallying cries in the subcontinent; just as Kant suggested, these ideals inspired and sustained for more than half a century the movement for independence from the British. But they also provoked, at the time of independence, a religious war in which a million people died and eleven million became refugees; it resulted in partition of the subcontinent and the establishment of the separate state of Pakistan as a homeland for the Muslim minority, who had carried on a parallel struggle within the larger independence movement for the right to determine *their* own destiny. Twenty-four years later, in 1971, they provoked a further partition of the subcontinent—this time of Pakistan, when its eastern wing broke away and established the separate state of Bangladesh as a homeland for the Bengali Muslims, who had begun agitating for the right to determine *their* own destiny. In fact, since independence there had hardly been a racial, religious, linguistic, tribal, or geographical group within the confines of the subcontinent some of whose members had not sent up a cry at one time or another for a separate homeland in the name of freedom and self-determination, and so posed a threat of further partition of the subcontinent into warring countries. For many of these separatists, Bangladesh became a paradigm of their struggle to win independence, even as the independence struggles of India and Pakistan were once the paradigm for Bangladesh's struggle.

In large measure, the Bangladesh movement for independence grew out of an erosion of democracy in Pakistan, which, in 1958, culminated in the establishment of a dictatorship under General Mohammad Ayub Khan. From the very beginning, Pakistan had been an uneasy alliance of two distinct cultural, economic, and linguistic entities (India, of course, is an uneasy alliance of dozens of such entities)—the richer Punjabis in the west and the poorer Bengalis in the east, separated by a thousand miles of Indian territory. The Punjabis of West Pakistan and the Bengalis of East Pakistan had much more in common with the Punjabis and Bengalis across the border in India than with each other; they were divided not only by geography but also by differences in language, in economic and social systems, in dress, and in diet. In fact, the only real bond between East Pakistan and West Pakistan was Islam, but, as other Muslim countries had discovered, religion alone could not bind together politically disparate entities. From the start, the Punjabis, who were much more prosperous than the Bengalis, ran Pakistan's Army, civil service, and industry. They strengthened and extended their advantage through the years until the nation's power and wealth became concentrated almost entirely in the west. The enmity with India, which had a negligible influence on the economy of West Pakistan, all but crippled the economy of East Pakistan, which, unlike West Pakistan, depended on India for trade. The Bengalis, who had come to feel exploited and subjugated, grew more and more restive, their predicament being particularly galling because they constituted a majority of Pakistan's population.

Initially, there was one thing besides religion which bound the two entities together, and that was their belief in a democratic form of government. Such a form of government did function, however crudely, for a time, and, through political representation, allowed for the expression and accommodation of some cultural differences. But Ayub's dictatorship ushered in a new order, which tried to institutionalize the economic and political dominance of West Pakistan over East Pakistan. (Almost from the start, many South Indians charged that Mrs. Gandhi's Emergency dictatorship was trying to institutionalize the economic and political dominance of the North over the South.) The avowed aims of Ayub's dictatorial rule (like those of Mrs. Gandhi's Emergency) were the stability and unity of Pakistan and the institution of paternalistic social and economic reforms, but in actuality his rule succeeded only in blocking change, entrenching feudalism, and repressing all cultural and political dissent. It thus inadvertently aided a separatist movement in East Pakistan.

The founding father of the Bengali separatist movement, Sheikh Mujibur Rahman—or simply Mujib—was born into a traditionally Muslim middle-class Bengali family in 1920. As a young man, he became caught up in the Indian freedom struggle. In the early years of Pakistan, he was a Pakistani patriot, but as the country moved toward dictatorship he came to feel that the government was becoming increasingly isolated from and unresponsive to the needs and wishes of his Bengali people and was devoting most of its energies to staying in power. He came to feel that East Pakistan had only substituted the rule of West Pakistan for the old rule of Britain—one colonial oligarchy for another. He helped to found the Awami League, a sort of people's movement, in East Pakistan, and in 1953 he became its general secretary. In the early years of its existence, the Awami League demanded merely that the Bengalis be given equal opportunity with the Punjabis—equal representation in the well-paying jobs of the civil and military bureaucracies, an equal share of foreign aid, and official use of the Bengali language. Pakistan's dictatorial government, instead of fulfilling these moderate demands, jailed the

Awami League leaders and redoubled its efforts at repression, through the use of martial law and emergency powers. As a result, Mujib himself spent a total of ten years in Pakistani jails. But the tightening of repression had the effect of making Mujib and the Awami League more radical and more popular. In fact, it was thanks in part to the Bengalis that Ayub Khan was forced to resign in 1969. As it turned out, Ayub was succeeded by an even more autocratic dictator, General Agha Muhammad Yahya Khan—who was, of course, from West Pakistan.

It was an attempt by General Yahya Khan to deal with some of these problems that precipitated the Bangladesh calamity. Apparently hoping to mollify the majority and to defuse what he regarded as a threat to the union of Pakistan, he decided, in 1969, to hand over his military government to civilian control, and in December of 1970 he allowed Pakistanis, for the first time in their twenty-three-year history, to vote—on the basis of universal male suffrage—for representatives to a constituent assembly. In the election, the Awami League, led by Mujib, campaigned openly for political and economic autonomy for East Pakistan, and won almost all the Bengali seats, while the Pakistan People's Party, led by the militant Zulfikar Ali Bhutto, was returned with a bare majority in West Pakistan. Once the election results had made it clear that the Awami League would dominate the constituent assembly—and, no doubt, the civilian government that emerged from it—Bhutto let it be known that he would not participate in any assembly or government in which West Pakistan and the Pakistan People's Party were not equal partners with East Pakistan and the Awami League. Mujib saw in Bhutto's stand only a design for perpetuating the "colonial subjugation" of East Pakistan by West Pakistan. General Yahya Khan seemed to be caught off guard by the strength of the democratic forces he had released. The election had unexpectedly turned into a referendum on East Pakistani autonomy, and when General Yahya Khan was actually confronted with the possibility that control might pass to the eager Bengali majority, he, like Bhutto, seemed unable to countenance any change in the relationship between East

Pakistan and West Pakistan, which might be the beginning of the end of the union. He therefore tried to get Mujib to moderate his demands, and, having failed, temporized by first delaying and then indefinitely postponing the inaugural session of the constituent assembly. General Yahya Khan insisted that he would not sacrifice the unity and integrity of the country, and rearrested Mujib and other leaders of the Awami League. He tried to impose a military solution on what was essentially a political problem. This tactic aroused protest in East Pakistan in early March of 1971, and he ordered his troops to shoot demonstrators; the shooting, in turn, led to an all-out Bengali civil-disobedience movement later in the month, and he gave his troops free rein, thus causing the death of perhaps as many as two hundred thousand Muslims and Hindus in the space of a few months. The repressive measures he took had no precedent in scale or severity under Ayub, let alone under the British. He practically wiped out the Bengali political and economic élite, and forced millions to flee to India. These measures, in effect, provoked a full-scale civil war, and they brought India into the fight on the side of East Pakistan, in the third Indo-Pakistani War.

In December, 1971, the war ended in the downfall of Yahya Khan and the creation of Bangladesh, with Pakistan losing fifty-five thousand square miles of its territory and half its population to the new country. The devastation of the Bengali homeland and the suffering of the Bengali people immediately became an international symbol of the tragic costs of independence, just as the devastation and suffering in India and Pakistan had been in 1947.

Mujib was released from his West Pakistan jail in an act of magnanimity by Yahya Khan's successor, Zulfikar Ali Bhutto, and returned home to a hero's welcome. He helped to establish a parliamentary democracy, like India's, in Bangladesh, and became its first Prime Minister. He tried to run the new nation according to the old democratic ideals of the Awami League, but he soon found that they were better suited, as he himself was, to the rhetoric of revolution than to the routine of administration. At first, he kept the doors of his house in Dacca, the capital of

Bangladesh, open at all times and dealt with suppliants and their problems by dispensing favors in the manner of a feudal land-owner, but he made little headway with his nation's social and economic problems. Increasingly frustrated, he closed his doors and began to surround himself with a private army, called Rakkhi Bahini, which had been formed after Bangladesh won its inde-pendence—a kind of personal paramilitary force. For a time, he continued to enjoy popular support, but his regime soon became notorious for nepotism and corruption. His sons and nephews were given positions of great power and influence, and much of the three billion dollars in aid supplied to the new country by the international community simply disappeared.

In December, 1974, Mujib assumed emergency powers and suspended civil liberties, and within a month he had so amended the democratic constitution as to emasculate it (much as Mrs. Gandhi was to do six months later). He had become a dictator, like Ayub Khan and Yahya Khan before him. Disillusionment with him and his government spread, and, in its most virulent form, infected the national Army. There were by then actually two armies in Bangladesh: the national Army, in the British apolitical tradition, and Mujib's small, private army, bound by personal loyalty to him, in the feudal tradition. The senior officers of the national Army, like their Indian counterparts, as a rule believed in civilian control, but they found Mujib's growing au-thoritarianism repugnant. The junior officers, moreover, greatly resented the increasing power of the Rakkhi Bahini, and many of them harbored personal grudges against Mujib. On August 6, 1975, a group of junior officers reportedly met in the house of Major Shariful Huq Dalim, in Dacca. Mujib had dismissed Dalim earlier in the year, apparently because of a quarrel between Dalim and a son of Ghazi Ghulam Mustaffa, a close associate of Mujib; the quarrel, it was said, dated back to a wedding party in the summer of 1974, when Mustaffa's son insulted Dalim's wife and Dalim slapped him across the face. The junior officers who gath-ered at Dalim's house were united by some such personal griev-ance against Mujib rather than by any common ideology or party membership. They decided to stage a coup, and in subsequent days they successfully enlisted the support of additional junior officers, who were angered by, among other things, a plan of Mujib's to dilute the power of the national Army by making each of the district governors—who had been appointed by Mujib and were loyal to him—the commandant of the Army and police units in his region.

The junior officers chose August 15th for their coup, for symbolic reasons: it was twenty-eight years to the day since the British had left the subcontinent. The officers moved their tanks and artillery pieces into Dacca from their military cantonment, a few miles away, and quickly surrounded the houses of Mujib and his most powerful relatives, Sheikh Falzul, Huq Moni, and Serniabat Abdur Rab, and also the headquarters of the Rakkhi Bahini, about twelve miles northwest of the city. Lewis Simons wrote in the Washington *Post:*

> According to some sources, the officer leading the troops at the president's house, a major named Huda, handed Mujib a document of resignation to sign. Mujib, in a characteristic outburst, refused and roundly abused the young officer.
>
> At that point, according to these same sources, one of Mujib's sons, Sheikh Jamal, burst into the room with a pistol in his hand and was shot dead. Mujib again cursed the officer. Then another son, Sheikh Kamal, stumbled into the room, shouting for help from the Rakkhi Bahini. Huda, armed with a Sten gun, cut down the son and his father.
>
> Then, as one source put it, "the real massacre began." Soldiers rushed into the house and began searching the rooms. In quick succession they opened fire on Mujib's wife, who was sobbing hysterically, their two new daughters-in-law, and their youngest son, ten-year-old Russell. The soldiers discovered Mujib's brother, Sheikh Nasser, hiding in a second-story bathroom and they stabbed him to death with bayonets. They also killed two servants.
>
> At Sheikh Moni's house . . . a tank opened fire and a large shell missed the building and impacted in the neighboring Mohammedpur section, killing a dozen people. The soldiers

also killed Moni's wife and child. . . . Rab was killed in his home and his wife was shot, too, but she reportedly survived and is hospitalized.

By dawn, the entire Mujib clan was dead.

The civilian government of Bangladesh technically continued in control for a brief time, but it did not dare punish Mujib's assassins, and was soon overthrown in another coup—this time by senior military officers, who ostensibly wanted to punish the assassins. Subsequently, there was still another coup. The causes both of Mujib's assassination and of these coups may have been more complex than the reports suggested, but Bangladesh was clearly in the grip of conspiratorial politics.

No poor country can be an ideal democracy. As Aristotle pointed out, "the natural elements" of democracy are middle-class citizens. Nehru's "adventure in democracy" was necessarily enjoyed mostly by the middle class, but he hoped that, with eventual improvement in the standard of living, the ranks of the middle class would swell, making possible a broader participation in the "adventure," and that with the passage of time the nascent democratic institutions would take hold, assuring India a stable and increasingly representative government. He felt that the democracy he led and nursed, for all its notorious corruption and inequities, and for all its crude and cumbersome ways, was the only real hope of keeping India's races, regions, religions, and cultures from fragmenting the country into dozens of warring factions and nations. He often looked across to Pakistan, citing its erosion of democracy and its military dictatorship as evidence justifying his fears and beliefs. In fact, the weight of the entire history of the subcontinent was on the side of war and division rather than on the side of unity and peace. As we have shown, within a few years of Nehru's death Pakistan, a much smaller and much more homogeneous country than India, became two antagonistic nations; of course, the causes of its breakup may have been as much geographical as they were political, but the civil war and the chaos that led up to it were directly traceable to the repressive policies of the dictatorship.

Within a few years more, Mrs. Gandhi launched her country upon the same all too familiar course, and before long there were signs that the drive for secession in South India, which the Indian democracy had managed to contain for many years, was again gathering strength, with the South Indians portraying her rule as domination by the North. And the South India movement was only the strongest of a number of secessionist movements that were afoot from east to west. Even if it were true, as Mrs. Gandhi and her apologists claimed, that to see the political form of government in India only in terms of human rights and civil liberties was to see India through Western eyes, still, no Indian who had lived through a bloody religious civil war and three wars with Pakistan within a quarter of a century or so could be blind to the dangers of sweeping dictatorships and further partitions.

# 9

# Mahatma Gandhi and Mrs. Gandhi

On May 18, 1974, Indira Gandhi's government detonated its first nuclear "device," about three hundred and thirty feet underground somewhere in the Rajasthan desert. Practically any country that could get hold of some plutonium could by then make its own nuclear "device," and India by its action weakened the political, moral, and psychological constraints that had restricted the use of nuclear weapons by the major powers—the United States, the Soviet Union, the United Kingdom, France, and China—and took the first step toward a possible proliferation of nuclear weapons among the minor powers. It was hard to imagine what set of priorities, what calculations, real or illusory, could have led the government of Mrs. Gandhi to join the nuclear club. The official explanation was that the "device" had no military significance and was part of a peaceful nuclear program to facilitate, among other things, earthmoving and the mining of ores. But the only difference between the peaceful and the military use of a nuclear "device" is the ability of a country to deliver it to a target, so the question of military significance was academic. Moreover, India has always had a large, indeterminable floating population of destitute men and women who, without any assistance from nuclear "devices," would, for the mere opportunity of gainful employment, move mountains.

The bizarre euphoria over the "device" among Indian politicians and journalists of every stripe was apparently produced by the fact that its successful detonation proclaimed India's military superiority to Pakistan and put China on notice that India was now capable of nuclear equality with it. But since 1971, when Pakistan lost the third Indo-Pakistani War, it had given many signs that it was prepared to reach an accommodation with India. And since 1962, when China voluntarily withdrew from the Indian territory it had won in the Sino-Indian War, it had given no indication of having territorial designs on India. At best, India gained a dubious psychological advantage over its old enemies. But it did so at the expense of world stability. The "device," it seemed, was intended to lend prestige at home to Mrs. Gandhi's hard-pressed government at a time when the country was confronting perhaps the worst food emergency in its history—yet nuclear "devices" could not grow wheat or rice. As a consequence of the food shortage in recent years, as many as two hundred million people, or one-third of India's population, have suffered permanent brain damage from malnutrition. One can get an idea of the Indira Gandhi government's scale of priorities from its budget between 1969 and 1974, when it spent a hundred and seventy-three million dollars on research and development of nuclear "devices," two hundred million dollars on housing, three hundred and seventy million dollars on family planning, and nine billion dollars directly on defense—two billion of it in 1973 alone.

India became a nuclear power in part because of an agreement reached in 1956 between the then Prime Minister of Canada, Louis St. Laurent, and the then Prime Minister of India, Jawaharlal Nehru. The agreement, under which Canada pledged to aid India in the development of nuclear energy for peaceful purposes, was, according to a report in the New York *Times,* prompted by Canada's realization that "the economic needs of India were so great that only the use of the most modern technology available could assist in raising the Indian standards of living within the time-frame seen by Nehru." Nehru was in this sense the heretic son of Mahatma Gandhi. Gandhi had a different "time-frame" for his country. He believed that for a poor country like India the road to economic development lay in an agrarian rather than an industrial revolution, and so over the years he developed a program for regenerating the bleak, disease-ridden villages in which most Indians live, by revitalizing the old relationships between the cultivator and the soil, the herdsman and his animals, the craftsman and his craft. His idea was simply to provide Indians with the opportunity to live in modest circumstances with a certain amount of dignity and decency—to make it possible for hundreds of millions who were going naked or in rags, were hungry or undernourished, and could find little or no work to be clothed, fed, and given useful occupations. This was Gandhi's Constructive Programme, his nonviolent revolution, which the Indian government, almost from the day of independence, summarily dismissed as utopian, without seriously testing it.

On November 10, 1948, General Omar Bradley, the Chief of Staff of the United States Army, said in Boston, "We have grasped the mystery of the atom and rejected the Sermon on the Mount. . . . Ours is a world of nuclear giants and ethical infants. We know more about war than we know about peace, more about killing than we know about living." Gandhi was, by contrast, a nuclear infant and an ethical giant, who tried to put the Sermon on the Mount into practice in his homeland. He tried to make of his life what he called "an experiment in nonviolence," and tried to learn and perfect the science of peace.

"Friends, we live in a country which is called Gandhi's land," the retired public servant M. C. Chagla said in his Ahmadabad speech. "Gandhiji . . . obtained . . . not merely freedom from the British government but also freedom from tyranny, oppression, injustice of every kind." Chagla said that Indira Gandhi had returned India to the old rule of tyranny, oppression, and injustice, but he added, "There is a saying in English that when the night is darkest the dawn is not far. I see the night very dark."

In truth, Mahatma Gandhi and Indira Gandhi personify two contrasting visions of what kind of country India should be. One vision has its source in the peasants, the other in the middle class. In spirit, one is democratic, the other élitist. In conception, one is agrarian, the other industrial. One depends on voluntary assent, the other on compulsion. One is so preoccupied with means that means and ends are practically identical (Mahatma Gandhi used to say, "I will not even get freedom for my country with evil means"), the other so preoccupied with ends that means hardly seem to matter (Indira Gandhi apparently would have stopped at nothing to eradicate poverty). One has continued to inspire dissent, and the other has more or less governed India since independence. One, though seemingly utopian, has modest goals, and the other, though seemingly realistic, has ambitious goals. The pre-Emergency constitution was itself a monument to this conflict. With one breath (Part III), it sanctified the right to property; with another (Part IV), it undermined that right. The preamble to the constitution declared that India was a sovereign democratic republic, established to secure for all its citizens social, economic, and political justice; liberty of thought, self-expression, faith, and worship; complete equality of status and opportunity; fraternity; human dignity; and so on. Such lofty objectives have hardly ever been attained, even in the richest countries. The conflict was inherent in, on the one hand, the reality of the abjectly poor, illiterate citizens for whom the letter of the constitution had no meaning and, on the other, the idealistic aspirations of the few well-to-do.

Although Mrs. Gandhi presented the Emergency as a daring attempt to resolve that conflict, she actually made it more acute, by expanding the gulf between the governed and the government. (In the opinion of the political scientist Miss Aloo Dastur, of the University of Bombay, the Emergency amendment putting the Prime Minister above the law in effect resurrected "the old discarded doctrine of the divine right of kings.") Mrs. Gandhi, of course, claimed that she was only using her limitless new powers to achieve Mahatma Gandhi's economic ends for the poor. But there is a great deal of difference between noble impulses and ignoble reality—for instance, between conferring legal rights on the serflike bonded peasants in order to protect them from landlords or moneylenders, which is what Mrs. Gandhi did, and actually giving those rights any force. Any illiterate bonded peasant who might have tried to avail himself of the legal machinery that she set up to help him would have risked losing his very livelihood, for that machinery, like the entire government, was run by people whose self-interest and class interest, of necessity, coincided with those of the landlords and moneylenders, the ones who had always dominated the villages, and could bribe an official or manufacture a charge against the peasant to get him arrested. The local forces of political power and oppression and the local forces of law and order continued to prop each other up. Given the class and caste structure of political parties, the administrative service, the Army, it was inevitable that their allies for winning votes, as for ruling the country under the Emergency, should be the rich and the middle peasantry, as Ashok Rudra contended in the final Emergency issue of *Seminar*.

Mrs. Gandhi and her Emergency only confirmed Mahatma Gandhi's fear that state power, frozen within existing colonial institutions like the élitist civil service, would degenerate into oppressive autocracy. Mahatma Gandhi felt that freedom, reform, and economic development required a complete decentralization and diffusion of power, that the government should be not separate from but an integral part of society, its power tempered by ethical and religious impulses. A monolithic bureaucracy, he believed, relied on compulsion, which only bred contempt and indifference, but participation by the greatest number in self-government offered hope for grass-roots education and self-concern. He felt that a peasant, however illiterate and impotent, was the best judge of his own needs, and that a government, however sophisticated and omnipotent, that was deaf to that peasant's voice and experience would ultimately fail.

Nirmal Verma, a follower of Mahatma Gandhi, wrote in that issue of *Seminar*:

In India, during the last two [or three] decades, those who had a predominant control over the media had no [intimate] experience of [the peasants'] suffering; those who really suffered had no word to express it. Despite all the noises that we made in the press and the Parliament, India remained a continent of silence.

[An] attachment to the right of full expression becomes merely formal and decorative unless it is transformed into the *moral concern* for the full articulation of man's total experience. That such a concern was singularly absent in our intelligentsia was revealed in the most cruel light when it so smoothly adjusted itself to the changed circumstances after the Emergency. . . .

But to infer from this, as our present rulers and some Marxists would like to infer, that liberty of expression, freedom of the press, and the basic right of a citizen to have free access to all the sources of information are mere "bourgeois values," which can be shelved for the sake of some mythical progress, is to fall a victim to another form of self-delusion. All projects of "revolutionary reform" may become instruments of oppression if the people for whom they are designed are deprived of the right to judge and comment upon them in the light of their experience. . . .

What is . . . common both to the affluent societies of the West [and] to the poor countries of the Third World is the supreme value which is attached to man's awareness of himself as a human being. No act of state power can be legitimate which violates this reality of awareness, forcing man to live in the "reality" of others, a censored reality, which is the other name for darkness.

Verma termed "sinister" the implication of Mrs. Gandhi that freedom of thought and expression was a bourgeois luxury for a poor country:

Sinister because it assumes that human beings living in poor societies are *less than human;* they may be fed and clothed *on the condition* that they cease to exercise their critical consciousness, cease to be human. . . .

But, apart from being sinister, such an argument negates itself in so far as it destroys the very conditions in which any radical reforms could be implemented. If reforms are for the people, the people should have free access to all the instruments through which they could make their experience available to the government.

One ancient instrument for expressing that experience of voiceless people was the *panchayat,* a sort of free-for-all get-together of the village men to air their quarrels and grievances without leaders, rules, agenda, or designated time or meeting place. The institution had long been subverted by the village landlord and moneylender, who had taken it over and run it—much as the country was taken over and run by Mrs. Gandhi's government during the Emergency. Moreover, in thirty years of modern middle-class rule in independent India the government, though it often gave lip service to the ideals of the *panchayat,* in actuality neglected to revive the *panchayat* in its true, lusty form. But on January 18, 1977, Mrs. Gandhi issued a call for "fresh elections," and with this call there were stirrings, which could not be neglected, of a different sort of national free-for-all. No matter what her calculations, she could not control the events she had set in motion. Thus, the nineteen months of the Emergency would later be remembered as an extraordinarily Orwellian passage of time in an ancient land.

# 10

# Risking Elections

Announcing the elections, Mrs. Gandhi observed, "Every election is an act of faith. It is an opportunity to cleanse public life of confusion. So let us go to the polls with the resolve to reaffirm the power of the people." She subsequently released most of the well-known political prisoners and suspended the press guidelines. Normally, state legislatures used to be dissolved simultaneously with Parliament, but in 1971 Mrs. Gandhi's government had so arranged matters that any future "general elections" could be restricted to the lower house of Parliament, with elections to state legislatures and their representative body, the upper house of Parliament, being "de-linked," and held later. Mrs. Gandhi's "fresh elections" were restricted to the lower house of Parliament and to Kerala, one of the few states that were not under Congress rule but in which Congress expected to do well. In any case, under the constitution, the elections for the lower house should have been held the previous March, when the Parliament's five-year mandate ran out. But in February, 1976, barely a month before they were due, she had the Parliament postpone them for a year; in November, 1976, she had the Parliament postpone them until November, 1977. Yet once the Emergency was under way she apparently had a great deal to gain by letting the elections take place according to the original schedule. She could have capitalized on the early dramatic economic benefits of the Emergency, which were always in danger of being cancelled by, for instance, a bad monsoon. She could have used the elections to revitalize the Congress Party from the grass roots, weeding out the dissident or ineffective elements by means of judicious dispensation of patronage and Party nominations, and so have made it an even stronger vehicle for personal power. She could have given Sanjay his opportunity to run for a seat then and win a political base of his own, and thus have averted the charges of an incipient Gandhi dynasty. She could have presented herself as a democrat rather than a dictator, and refurbished her image abroad, for it is thought that, contrary to her public protestations, she was very sensitive to Western criticism. She and her government, increasingly insulated from the people, could have informed themselves about the mood of the country while providing a safety valve for pent-up grievances. Elections would also have had the effect of smoking out the opposition that had gone underground, and would have given her and her intelligence network a chance to take their true measure. As a constitutional dictator, she could then have easily exploited the incumbent's traditional advantages of office, power, and money. The Congress Party would almost certainly have been reëlected, as it had been in all the elections since independence. Her victory at the polls, in addition to washing away the stain of her conviction, would have legitimized her Emergency powers and all the Emergency laws and constitutional amendments. At the same time, her government would have been given a reprieve from further electoral challenges for five years, which would have permitted it to suspend, or even lift, the Emergency without any diminution in her authority.

Even then, of course, Mrs. Gandhi would have run certain risks. She might have set off defection movements in her party whenever elections were held, for it had always encompassed a spectrum of political views from extreme right to extreme left, and conflicts between warring, opportunistic leaders had always threatened to erupt; but at the start of 1976 the Party members would have taken it for granted that she was their best hope at the polls, and most of them would doubtless have stayed with her. To give the elections a semblance of fairness, she would have had to release political prisoners, suspend press censorship, and expose herself to vituperative attacks; but the repercussions of such measures would probably have had only a nuisance value then, which she would have been able to combat by depicting her opponents as destructive, subversive, and calumnious—and, anyway, politicians and journalists could have been kept in line by the threat of arrests and rearrests. Some of the newly elected members of Parliament might have proved strident, and she would not have been able to arrest them immediately following the elections; but after a proper grace period she could probably have proceeded against them. If she had then eventually permitted elections for the state legislatures, the opposition parties might have won majorities in some states, as in the past, and she would have had trouble dismissing these opposition state governments peremptorily; but she had bided her time with such governments before, and she could no doubt have done so again.

The fact remains that, despite many gains and few risks, she had apparently decided not to hold even Parliamentary elections until 1977. Her January announcement that elections would be held two months later set observers to puzzling over what could have happened since February of 1976—or, more probably, since November of that year—to change her mind. Did her success with the Forty-fourth Amendment to the constitution (it actually became part of the Forty-second Amendment), on which she permitted a modicum of free debate and free reporting, give her new confidence? Did she, in fact, intend that debate to be a test run for the elections? Were the economic conditions seen to be at their peak? (By January, 1977, India, in addition to large stocks of food grains, had sizable reserves of foreign exchange and a surplus in the budget.) Or, alternatively, had they suddenly started deteriorating? (The January action of the Organization of Petroleum Exporting Countries in raising the price of oil intensified inflationary pressures, and retail prices had already risen ten per cent since the previous March.) Did she have some knowledge, through her intelligence network, of restiveness in the Army or in the middle-class establishment? Did a reported rift with the pro-Soviet Communists over Sanjay and her crackdown on the left make her think better of her regime's increasing dependence on the Soviet Union? Had the backlash against certain of her Emergency programs, like sterilization, made her wish for a mandate? Was she afraid that she would forfeit a certain amount of flexibility if she did not call the elections soon? (Because of the climate and problems of communication, elections are really feasible in India only in the spring.) Was she being emotionally blackmailed by Sanjay? Had she been unaware of the restiveness in her party—perhaps exacerbated by Sanjay's emergence as the heir apparent—and so overestimated her hold on it? (She was apparently "astounded" when, soon after her election announcement, her Minister of Agriculture, Jagjivan Ram, defected from the Party and founded a splinter Congress group, called the Congress for Democracy, to fight for her defeat.) Had she lost faith in the ability of her Emergency powers to bring about an economic miracle? Did she have some regrets about proclaiming the Emergency in the first place? The explanation, some observers concluded, might be no more complicated than that she had all along been secretly planning to announce the elections at this late date with the aim of catching her opposition off guard.

In contrast with the Congress Party, which had the political stage to itself for nineteen months, and time to prepare for elections, to build up the Party machine, and to fill the Party coffers—with leading industrialists vying with each other to back the regime—the non-Communist opposition parties had been condemned to political inactivity. With their leaders and politicians imprisoned and silenced, their party organizations had been dispersed and their sources of party funds dried up. A motley collection, embracing socialist ideologies, laissez-faire capitalism, and militant Hindu chauvinism, these parties had suddenly been given a bare two months to organize, to agree on a common platform, to raise campaign money, to come up with five hundred and forty-two candidates for Parliament (the number of Parliamentary constituencies had increased by about twenty seats since the last election), and somehow to make them known to the three hundred and twenty million qualified voters, who would be polled in about three hundred and forty-three thousand voting booths. To be elected, each candidate had to get his message across to hundreds of thousands of poor, illiterate constituents.

The fact that these parties agreed to participate in the elections at all, and without insisting that the Emergency be lifted first—if only as a gesture of good faith—was in its way at least as puzzling as the calling of the elections by Mrs. Gandhi, whose whole political career had been highlighted by bold tactical moves.

# 11

# The Vote

In March of 1977, the Orwellian state of Indira Gandhi came to an end, in a manner that no one, least of all the author of "Nineteen Eighty Four," could have prophesied. The end of that state is the most hopeful sign in recent years for the growth of democracy in a poor country.

India's sixth general elections were held between the sixteenth and the twentieth of March. At the start of the campaign, the impression that the elections were another political ploy to disarm her opponents and to fortify her position as a constitutional dictator was strengthened when it was learned that Sanjay would stand for election as a Congress Party candidate from the constituency of Amethi. Amethi was in the shadow of Mrs. Gandhi's constituency, Rae Bareli, and, like Rae Bareli, was considered entirely "safe," since it was in Uttar Pradesh, the traditional power base of both the Nehrus and the Congress Party. Not surprisingly, everyone concerned took it for granted that the elections would serve only to expose the impotence of the electorate, partly because they were to be held under Mrs. Gandhi's "relaxed enforcement" of the Emergency—which in fact amounted to another brand of emergency, one without sanction in the constitution. Article 352 provided that the government could proclaim an emergency in the event of or in anticipation of "external aggression or internal disturbance." Since Mrs. Gandhi had only relaxed, not revoked, the Emergency, she must have concluded that the conditions that led her to institute the Emergency were still in existence; but if those conditions were still in existence, then she was wrong to relax the Emergency, and if they were not still in existence, then she was wrong to continue the Emergency in any form. (And, of course, if they had never been in existence, she had been wrong to institute the Emergency in the first place.) She could not have it both ways, and, partly for that reason, the opposition, after she announced the elections, agitated to get Mrs. Gandhi to revoke the Emergency. The effort failed, so the opposition was obliged to fight the elections under less than ideal conditions. In Mrs. Gandhi's view, though, the elections were being conducted only "less unfreely."

During the campaign, there was much political euphoria over the formation of the Janata Party, a coalition of most of the major non-Communist opposition parties: the old-guard splinter of the Congress which Mrs. Gandhi had routed in 1969; Bharatiya Lok Dal, or People's Party; Jana Sangh; and the Socialist Party. (Many minor parties, especially regional ones, made informal alliances with Janata or Congress and nominated their own candidates.) For the first time, there was a formidable array of opposition, and it had clear-cut campaign issues in, among other things, Mrs. Gandhi's burgeoning dictatorship and Sanjay's dynastic pretensions. Furthermore, the leaders of the opposition included some of the more illustrious names in Indian politics. There was Vijaya Lakshmi Pandit—sister of Jawaharlal Nehru and aunt of Mrs. Gandhi—who, unlike her daughter Nayantara Sahgal, had kept silent during the Emergency, but who now invoked the memory of her brother and of Mahatma Gandhi to rebuke her niece. ("When the Emergency is the law of the land and one by one all the freedoms that are considered essential to the growth of democracy are suffocated, I thought I would be at peace with myself if I did what little I am able to do at this age—I am now seventy-six. . . . I remember Mahatma Gandhi took up the people of India in his hands when they were less than pygmies and he made giants out of them. Now . . . those giants have been reduced to pygmies.") There was Morarji Desai, who, perhaps more than anyone else in Indian politics, was associated in the minds of the people with Mahatma Gandhi's principles. There was Jagjivan Ram, who had the distinction of having been a Cabinet Minister almost continuously since independence, until his resignation from Mrs. Gandhi's Cabinet and the Congress Party. Then, there was Jaya Prakash Narayan, who had come increasingly to wield spiritual influence over the country.

Yet the political euphoria seemed to be based on wishful thinking. The Janata Party had been formed so hastily from the decimated ranks of the opposition parties (which had been all but destroyed by the Emergency), and included politicians of such disparate ideologies, and was so deficient in organization and money, that it was hard to imagine its surviving the campaign, let alone having the ability to win the elections or to govern the country. And, however compelling the political issues at stake, the opposition had barely two months to get its message across to the three hundred and twenty million voters, most of them dispersed over more than half a million villages. Then, the sudden death, in February, of President Fakhruddin Ali Ahmed curtailed political activities for several days, so the time left for campaigning was still shorter. Even the strength of the opposition leadership was deceptive. Mrs. Pandit was less well known as a politician at home than she was as a diplomat abroad, for she had served as High Commissioner in England, and as Ambassador to the Soviet Union, the United States, and the United Nations. Morarji Desai was so rigid in his adherence to the puritanical principles of Gandhi's thought that he had few supporters in the political and military establishment; besides, he was eighty-one years old and was a member of the routed old Congress. Jagjivan Ram, although formally a member of Mrs. Gandhi's Congress "new guard," was actually a holdover from the old Congress. All along, he had been a token Untouchable in the government, tolerated, and even courted, because of his powerful political constituency of the hundred million Untouchables rather than for any special administrative talent or intellectual ability. There was also a touch of political scandal about him. For nearly ten years, he had failed to pay any income tax; when he was caught, in 1969, he claimed that it was an oversight. Mrs. Gandhi publicly forgave him for his "forgetfulness." (In 1966, he had been possibly the decisive force in Mrs. Gandhi's election as Prime Minister.) Jaya Prakash Narayan was by then so sick that he campaigned at the risk of his life, and in the last days before the elections was forced to cancel all his political engagements.

Further, the "relaxed" aspect of Mrs. Gandhi's "relaxed enforcement" of the Emergency struck some Indian observers as more apparent than real. For example, she claimed that she was releasing all political prisoners, and, indeed, the immediate release of well-known prisoners gave an impression of good faith, but it soon became clear that many of the lesser-known state and district political workers were not being released. When the Janata leaders confronted Mrs. Gandhi with this anomaly, asking how there could be "free elections" when some of the political workers were unfree, she hedged; the state authorities were probably negligent in carrying out her orders, she said, or else the political workers concerned must actually have been imprisoned for hoarding or black-marketing, and so were never eligible for release. Although many of these lesser-known prisoners were eventually released, others were not, and some of them held a twenty-four-hour hunger strike a few days before the elections to dramatize their plight. Jaya Prakash Narayan, protesting the continued detention of such prisoners, went as far as to call the supposed relaxation of the Emergency and the holding of the elections "a mockery."

In the second week of March, there were reports that Mrs. Gandhi's government was moving the Border Security Force and the Central Reserve Police to district headquarters throughout the country. These reports gave rise to fears that Mrs. Gandhi intended to rig the election, as Prime Minister Zulfikar Ali Bhutto had just done in Pakistan (and perhaps to overturn the results if they went against her). Bhutto had announced elections there a few days before Mrs. Gandhi made her announcement; indeed, it was said that Bhutto had shamed her into holding elections, because if he, an obvious dictator, could risk elections, how could she, a professed democrat, avoid them? Pakistan held its elections on the seventh of March. Two hundred seats for Parliament were at stake, and Bhutto's government declared that the ruling Pakistan People's Party had won most of the seats; the principal opposition leader, Air Marshal Asghar Khan, immediately charged that the election had been "rigged on a very massive scale" (and neutral commentators largely concurred). Weeks of riots in the major cities of Pakistan followed, and the riots were being ruthlessly suppressed by heavy deployment of the police.

Mrs. Gandhi's own conduct during the campaign was less than reassuring. She often said she would "abide by the verdict" of the elections—as if, in truly democratic elections, she would have any choice. She repeatedly defended herself against the charge of being a dictator by saying that dictators don't hold elections—although, as the opposition pointed out, Hitler, for one, held a free election after he became Chancellor of Germany. (And, of course, there was Bhutto.) She also resorted to economic blandishments. For instance, instead of letting each state go on allocating its own food supplies, she converted the entire country into a single food zone; the new scheme meant that states enjoying food surpluses now had to share with states suffering food shortages—something she was able to arrange without alienating the surplus-food states because the two excellent monsoons had resulted in a general abundance of food in the country. The English-language Indian daily the *Statesman,* discussing these blandishments, commented wryly that the Central Election Commission's "stipulation that 'the ruling party should ensure that no cause is given for any complaint that it has used its official position for the purposes of its election campaign' is not best observed with a gift package that makes Lloyd George's notorious sale of honours look like an amateurish exercise in winning friends and influencing people."

Mrs. Gandhi's advisers had let it be publicly known at the outset that she planned to use the occasion of the elections to revitalize the Congress Party and turn it into a more effective instrument of her power. They had made it clear that her intentions were to get rid of tired old Party veterans, who had gone on representing Parliamentary constituencies because of their entrenched positions among their constituents, and to replace these veterans with lusty new blood from the youth wing of the Congress, which Sanjay had now headed for some months. In fact, her advisers had said that as many as half of the candidates for Parliament would be selected from the youth wing. But when, after calling the elections, she discovered, to her utter amazement, that she would have to confront not only a united opposition but also a powerful new dissident faction of her own party under Jagjivan Ram, she hastily revamped her entire election strategy. She all but ignored Sanjay's untried young recruits in the scramble to get every last one of the battle-tested veterans to stand for Parliament.

Once the Congress and the other parties had chosen their candidates, the campaign began in earnest. Mrs. Gandhi restricted Sanjay's political activities mostly to Amethi, while she herself, in the space of twenty-seven days, from February 17th to March 15th, campaigned in practically every one of the twenty-two states, addressing two hundred and twenty-four public meetings—something of a record for any politician. Throughout the campaign, she and the Congress Party sounded an apocalyptic theme; for instance, a Party statement issued in the final days of the campaign declared, "There is no alternative to the Congress. The alternative, if alternative it can be called, is a dangerous and explosive combination of incompatibles of extreme ideologies which, if given power, could explode the nation and finish once and for all the great purposes upon which we are embarked." (The Janata Party and the Congress for Democracy sounded an equally apocalyptic theme; for instance, Jaya Prakash Narayan stated, also in the final days of the campaign, "This is the last chance. If you falter now, nineteen months of tyranny shall become years of terror.")

Since the previous elections, in 1971, about three hundred thousand officials had spent a total of nine months preparing new electoral rolls, which had to be constantly brought up to date, because the electorate had grown by about fifty million. At least two million additional government officials had to be mobilized to man about three hundred and seventy-three thousand polling stations. The actual process of taking the poll was even more cumbersome. Because of the country's primitive communications system, the polling had to be spread over five days. (In the northern states of Jammu and Kashmir, and Himachal Pradesh, some remote constituencies were snowbound, and voters there could not cast their ballots until late May or June.) Because seventy per cent of the electorate was unable even to affix a signature to a voters' list, special precautions had to be taken to insure fair elections. Ballots with a complicated system of serial numbers were printed to serve as a safeguard against the use of counterfeit ballots. At polling stations (and sometimes a polling station was no more than a ballot box behind a blackboard or a bed sheet), in order to prevent a voter from voting twice, his left index finger was marked with ink that could not be washed off for about a week. ("The system of applying an indelible ink mark on the index finger of the left hand of a voter before he casts his vote has been improved upon by the Election Commission," observed the *Statesman*. "The mark will now be applied to the root of the nail and any attempt at removing it would be a painful and difficult exercise.") Each voter was given a pre-inked rubber stamp with an "X" on it, and a paper ballot prominently displaying party ideographs—a cow and calf for the Congress Party, for instance, and a peasant with a plow over his shoulder for the Janata Party—and was instructed how to stamp the ideograph of his choice in secret and drop the ballot in the ballot box, which had previously been sealed with countersignatures of government officials and the agents of the various parties. The balloting at each polling station was overseen by officials from the central government and by party agents. Additional measures also had to be taken, against harassment and intimidation of the voters, and against so-called booth-capturers—political workers, from a party that expected to lose, who would raid polling stations, stamp the ideograph of their party on all the ballots, and then stuff them in the ballot box. (In the event of a successful booth capture, provisions were made for taking a fresh vote.) After the polls closed, each ballot box had to be taken to a storage place, where the ballots were counted. For transporting the boxes, the government had to make available as many as a hundred vehicles in a constituency.

In previous elections, the opposition parties collectively had received a popular vote far in excess of their actual representation in Parliament. Even in 1971, when Mrs. Gandhi and her party, riding the crest of her anti-Pakistan, pro-Bangladesh policy, were returned with one of their greatest majorities ever, winning three hundred and forty-nine seats, or two-thirds of the seats in Parliament (they later won still larger representation in the states), a coalition of four parties, which constituted her main opposition in the elections, together won twenty-two per cent of the popular vote, but only forty-eight, or less than a tenth, of the seats in Parliament. In fact, the Congress Party had not managed to obtain fifty per cent of the popular vote in any general elections. It was because the opposition parties had always run candidates against each other, splitting the vote among themselves, that they had remained powerless. In this year's elections, however, the opposition parties for the most part agreed not to run candidates against each other, and most of the contests were "straight fights" between the Congress and one or another of the opposition parties.

The results were unprecedented. Sixty per cent of the electorate, or about a hundred and ninety-four million people, voted. The Janata Party received about forty-three per cent of the ballots, or about eighty-four million votes; and the Congress Party received about thirty-five per cent of the ballots—the lowest percentage since independence—or about sixty-five million votes. In terms of Parliamentary representation, out of five hundred and forty-two seats, the Janata Party won two hundred and seventy, the Congress Party one hundred and fifty-three, the Congress for Democracy twenty-eight, the pro-Chinese (and pro-Janata) Communists twenty-two, and the pro-Soviet (and pro-Mrs. Gandhi) Communists seven—the balance of the seats going to sundry others, including seven independents. Mrs. Gandhi was overwhelmingly defeated in Rae Bareli by her longtime foe Raj Narain. Sanjay Gandhi and practically every important Minister and adviser of Mrs. Gandhi's were also defeated in their individual contests for Parliament. On the other hand, even George Fernandes, one of Mrs. Gandhi's most hated enemies, who had fought for a seat in Parliament from a jail cell, where he was awaiting trial on charges of criminal conspiracy to overthrow the government by violence, was victorious. By midafternoon of March 20th, many Indian observers knew the irreversible direction of the election results, but the facts were somehow kept from Mrs. Gandhi until eight o'clock that evening. Upon learning them, she went into seclusion. The next morning at four, she drove to the residence of B. D. Jatti, who had been acting President since Fakhruddin Ali Ahmed's death, and asked him to revoke the twenty-one-month-old Emergency. It was her penultimate official act, followed almost at once by her resignation.

Morarji Desai succeeded her as Prime Minister, and one week later his new government revoked the earlier, "external" state of emergency, which had been proclaimed at the outbreak of the Bangladesh war. The new government also announced in Parliament that it intended to repeal all the Emergency laws and constitutional amendments. Any repeal of a constitutional amendment, however, would require concurrence of two-thirds of the state legislatures and also of the upper house of Parliament; and, because of the 1971 "de-linking," the state legislatures and the upper house continued under Congress rule, so that the new government, despite its announced intentions, was in no position to rid the country of the Emergency, root and branch, on the spot.

Within a few months, the new government was in fact able to hold elections in many of the states, and it won in most of them, but the membership of the upper house could change only gradually, over a period of years.

Mrs. Gandhi and her party were turned out of office primarily by the poor. No one has been able to explain exactly how the poor seized the election as an occasion for rebelling against their Ma-Bap, especially since they had to reject the propaganda of All-India Radio. (Most of them by that time had access to transistors.) But then the rumors—a blend of fact and fiction—about the dire effects of the Emergency on the poor had for some time been travelling rapidly through the villages by word of mouth. It was rumored, for instance, that the government was using the Emergency as an excuse to demolish the hutments of the poor, with the homeless poor being shipped out to prison labor camps in the desert—a rumor based on Sanjay's "beautification of the cities." It was also rumored that the government was using the Emergency to drive rice, wheat, lentils, cooking oil, and soap off the market. In reality, such necessities had become scarce because their prices were held down during the Emergency. It was said that the country was being run by "the boy"—people's derisive term for Sanjay—while venerated elders were in jail. In the years of the freedom struggle against the British raj, the poor had learned that the government could personify vice and that jail could personify virtue, and that a politician's most important credential could be his jail sentence, for there was hardly a major politician who had not once served some time in a British jail. Above all, it was rumored that "the boy" was using the Emergency to castrate the poor much as village bulls were castrated to make bullocks—a rumor based on Sanjay's sterilization program. The villagers understood very little about the effects of vasectomies—hastily performed as they were by the government, with regard only for statistics. Superstitiously, people associated sterilization with sexual impotence, emasculation, and loss of life-giving energy and spiritual strength—an assault on their bodies, their families, and their religions. Relatively few of the poor had direct experience of vasectomies, but it seemed that a great many of them had heard of people who had undergone the operation and suffered disastrous consequences. "Congressmen are finding it hard to counter the Janata Party propaganda that if the Congress is returned to power, *nasbandi* [vasectomy] will be intensified," wrote a correspondent for the *Statesman* shortly before the elections. "Over the past two weeks this 'wave' has taken the form of a scare. . . . Yet in Rae Bareli villages, people talk of excesses in Amethi, in Amethi, they speak of Sultanpur, and so on." In the past, the *sarpanch* (headman) of the *panchayat,* a villager himself, who was often a Congress Party worker, had been able to counteract damaging rumors and sway the votes of the village to the Congress camp, sometimes by actually buying and selling these votes, trading government favors for village pledges. The program for forced sterilization was so closely identified with Sanjay, however, that the political effectiveness of the *sarpanch* was undermined, as was that of Mrs. Gandhi herself. At the polls, the lines of the poor were longer, and there were larger numbers of frightened-looking men and women in them, than in any previous elections. Certainly a poor villager understood the meaning of the choice between dictatorship and democracy, between Emergency measures and democratic procedures, if only, perhaps, from his daily experience with the local constable and other petty officials. During the Emergency, these government functionaries, with no legal checks on their power, had become increasingly remote and arbitrary, exacerbating the villagers' customary fear of authority.

Oddly, the only precedent for the role of rumor in Mrs. Gandhi's upset may have been its role in the Indian Mutiny of 1857. One of the main causes of that mutiny was a rumored offense to the religious sensibilities of the Hindu and Muslim sepoys. At the time, British military authorities had introduced new rifles, which used greased cartridges, and the troops were instructed to bite off the ends of the cartridges when loading. It was rumored among the Hindus that the cartridges were greased with the fat of sacred cows, and among the Muslims that the same cartridges were greased with the fat of forbidden pigs. Both Hindus and Muslims came to believe that these cartridges were part of a British plot to force them to put the cartridges in their mouths in order to make them into outcastes or infidels, and so easy prey for Christian missionaries. The British authorities, in their ignorance, had indeed failed to take the elementary precaution of not using cow or pig fat. Mysteriously, chapatties (small unleavened cakes) were distributed from village to village, from district to district, across the lowlands and highlands of India, as a signal to the people to rebel. This improvised means of communication touched off the great Mutiny and led to the transfer of the Indian government from the East India Company to the British crown.

In retrospect, Mrs. Gandhi's defeat can be interpreted in many ways: The election had only a negative significance; the people were rejecting the program of Mrs. Gandhi, not necessarily affirming that of the opposition. Mrs. Gandhi had to fail, because she was trying to reconcile two contradictory propositions—that a poor country needs an imposed dictatorial government, and that this government, after it has been imposed, can be democratically elected. Mrs. Gandhi was naïve in believing that the poor would not be able to see through the smoke screen of the Emergency. Mrs. Gandhi was a casualty of India's thirty-year-old tradition of elections by secret ballot; of the strict electoral law under which she herself had been convicted of electoral irregularities; and of the elaborate procedures involving independent observers at every stage and a supervisory Central Election Commission. As a result, even if she had wanted to, she could not have rigged the elections—as Zulfikar Ali Bhutto presumably did—by having the ballot boxes stuffed in secret. Or, at least, she would have needed the coöperation of local constables and other petty officials, but she had forfeited their support—along with the support of their caste and religious leaders—by her actions during the Emergency, and they had increasingly functioned as a law unto themselves, beholden neither to Mrs. Gandhi nor to the villagers.

Some find the sources of Mrs. Gandhi's downfall in her character—specifically, in her overreaching vanity, in her hubris. She was brought up to think of herself as special, set apart by birth from the Indian masses. When she became Prime Minister, she presented herself as someone predestined to be the ideal leader, and, following her father's example, she encouraged people to think of her as the great leader of the world's greatest democracy. She fostered talk about the fact that she was a Nehru, a rational "modern mind" in a country of medieval superstition. After the proclamation of the Emergency, it was clear from her speeches that she didn't feel comfortable in the role of self-appointed dictator and yearned to be a constitutional dictator. She often claimed that India's problems had forced her onto the dictatorial road, but with her panoply of Emergency laws and constitutional amendments she succeeded only in weakening the legitimacy of her rule. However she justified her actions to the world, she could not escape her Nehru heritage, including her Nehru conscience. (Did she sometimes ask herself "What would Papu say?" as she jailed his friends and colleagues?) In her speeches during the Emergency, she dwelt increasingly on her childhood memories: how she had always been the leader of her playmates; how she had burned her English-made doll; how she had been in the vanguard of charges in imaginary battles; how she had been the first in a group to reach the top of a mountain; how she had dreamed of growing up to be a Joan of Arc. In any case, it seemed that she was never at peace with herself. During the first years of her Prime Ministership, she liked to present herself as a Westernized Indian—as a patron of Western arts in India, and as a cosmopolitan hostess who was as much at home with Westerners as she was with Indians—but lately she had begun to strike out against the West, condemning it as a meddling, decadent, materialistic society. She had started portraying herself as a devout Hindu. She would go with her head demurely covered to do obeisance to holy men and to have an audience with her guru, Anandamayi Ma—or simply Ananda—the Bengali mystic whose followers believe her to be an incarnation of Kali, the goddess of destruction, or even of Sarasvati, the goddess of speech itself. Of course, it is hard to say whether Mrs. Gandhi's volte-face was a matter of political expedience or of political conviction, or was simply the expression of her feelings of guilt, or was an attempt to attain some degree of moral consistency. She was renowned for her cunning; she had outwitted all of her father's colleagues, some of the wisest old tortoises of Indian politics. And she was now hoist with her own petard. Who would have thought that the figure of Nemesis would appear to Nehru's daughter in the guise of Parliamentary elections?

It was a split in her own Congress Party in 1975 that forced Mrs. Gandhi onto the dictatorial route of proclaiming the Emergency. Now, in a sense, another split in that party had forced her out of power, and seemingly eliminated her chances of ever again holding high office. Strangely, her successor, Morarji Desai, was known to be by inclination the most autocratic man in Indian politics. In fact, his authoritarianism was largely responsible for his defeat by Mrs. Gandhi for the office of Prime Minister in 1966, when he was her main rival. Similarly, in 1969 his authoritarianism deepened the split between the old and the new guards in the Congress which consolidated Mrs. Gandhi's position as Prime Minister and seemingly eliminated *his* chances of ever again holding high office.

A friend in New Delhi wrote shortly after the elections:

I hope you were able, in New York, to follow the campaign in the *desi* [native] newspapers and magazines. The *Statesman* and the *Indian Express* did a superb job; the *Times of India* woke up as the polling approached; the *Hindustan Times* was futile; but *Seminar* resumed publication and brought out two very forthright issues. It's been a fantastic election and the results have been greeted with a jubilation reminiscent of Independence Day. So far, people are not being boorish or vindictive about Mrs. Gandhi's defeat—the atmosphere here is just infectiously merry. And Jaya Prakash

Narayan, like a latter-day Mahatma Gandhi, is keeping the Janata Party sober and giving it the sort of vision that governments here have lacked since independence. Let's see what the Janata Party does—but at present we feel happy and hopeful. The electorate has proved that no government can afford to trample on us—"We, the people of India"—with impunity.

The election-counting days were quite exhausting. Every night, we would go to bed at one thirty in the morning and wake up at five thirty. To get the latest scoop on the election results, we would rush over to Uncle Romesh's, on Pandara Road. Everyone at Pandara Road voted Janata—truly remarkable, considering our family's long history of government service.

All-India Radio lived up to expectation, by not reporting the Congress disasters even as they were happening. The crowd had to swarm around newspaper and party offices all day and night for the latest information. Big scoreboards were put up at Connaught Circus, Bahadur Shah Zafar Marg, etc., giving the latest election figures, and you should have seen the crowds—restrained but merry. Our two-year-old daughter, Leela, of course, was merrier than anyone. On the first counting day, she had as many as three drives in the evening—to the various newspaper and party offices and scoreboards—and confidently declared *"Pupup, main elections se bari khush hoon."* ["Papa, I am very happy with the elections."] It's marvellous to be free of the Emergency: press censorship, Sanjay—not to mention Bansi Lal, V. C. Shukla, H. R. Gokhale, and all the other Congress rogues. Even nice old Swaran Singh, who chaired the notorious Committee to rewrite the Constitution for legitimizing the burgeoning dictatorship, has bit the dust. (Can you believe that now George Fernandes is the Minister of Communications, and Raj Narain the Minister of Health?) I think people are sorry for Mrs. G., as I am, but, as Aunt Mala says, supposedly quoting from the Ramayana, "Where your advisers don't tell you the truth, there is no hope for good government." On the last night of the counting, we were too tired to go out, but the whole family from Pandara Road arrived at our door and we never went to bed.

People here are less interested in who the new Prime Minister is and in what he is like than I expect people outside India are—it's enough to have got rid of one and shown that no one is so exalted as to be deified, even a Prime Minister or a Nehru. For the first time, I think, one sees poor *desis* as free men with respect for themselves and their own judgment rather than blind faith in government office-holders.

Since the letter was written, there has been such an onrush of material and testimony—most of it formless or contradictory—about things that happened during the Emergency that it will be years before anyone can hope to sift through it. Yet, whatever the eventual judgment, *"Pupup, main elections se bari khush hoon"* may turn out to be as good an epitaph as any for Mrs. Gandhi's Orwellian state.

# Index

# Index

*Penguin Classics*

## THE BHAGAVAD GITA
*Translated by Juan Mascaró*

The eighteen chapters of the *Bhagavad Gita* (c. 500 B.C.), the glory of Sanskrit literature, encompass the whole spiritual struggle of a human soul, and the three central themes of this immortal poem—Love, Light, and Life—arise from the symphonic vision of God in all things and of all things in God.

## THE DHAMMAPADA
*Translated by Juan Mascaró*

The *Dhammapada* is a collection of aphorisms which illustrate the Buddhist *dhamma*, or moral system. Probably compiled in the third century B.C., the verses deal with the struggle towards Nirvana—the supreme goal for the Buddhist—and point out the narrow Path of Perfection which leads to it.

## THE UPANISHADS
*Translated and selected by Juan Mascaró*

*The Upanishads* represent for the Hindu approximately what the New Testament represents for the Christian. The earliest of these spiritual treatises, which vary greatly in length, were put down in Sanskrit between 800 and 400 B.C. This selection from twelve Upanishads reveals the paradoxical variety and unity, the great questions and the simple answers, the spiritual wisdom and romantic imagination of these "Himalayas of the Soul."

## HINDU MYTHS
*Translated by Wendy O'Flaherty*

This new selection of seventy-five seminal myths spans the wide range of classical Indian sources, from the serpent-slaying Indra of the Vedas (c. 1200 B.C.) to the medieval pantheon—the phallic and ascetic Siva, the maternal and bloodthirsty Goddess, the mischievous child Krishna, the other avatars of Vishnu, and the many minor gods, demons, rivers, and animals sacred to Hinduism.

Some other books published by Penguin
are described on the following page.

# Index